Photograhy by Ray Main

caroline murphy

101 IDEAS

bathrooms

quadrille

Editorial Director Jane O'Shea
Art Director Helen Lewis
Designer Paul Welti
Project Editor Hilary Mandleberg
Production Jane Rogers

Photography Ray Main

First published in 2004 by
Quadrille Publishing Limited
Alhambra House
27–31 Charing Cross Road
London WC2H 0LS

British Library Cataloguing-in-Publication
Data. A catalogue record for this book is
available from the British Library.

ISBN 1 84400 087 7

Every effort has been made to ensure the
accuracy of the information in this book. In no
circumstances can the publisher or the author
accept any liability for any loss, injury or
damage of any kind resulting from any error in
or omission from the information contained in
this book.

Printed and bound in China

contents

part one
the big picture

part one

the big picture

1 bathroom basics

10 elements

Designing a bathroom may seem a daunting task. The technicalities of plumbing, worries about waterproofing, the upheaval of structural change . . . there are so many practical matters to consider. Yet simultaneously, designing a bathroom can be fun. Imagine making that 'if I won the lottery . . .' wish-list, poring over brochures filled with beautiful bathrooms, unleashing creative instincts you never knew you had. You could really enjoy the rewarding visual aspects of bathroom design (and hand the complex technical side to the experts).

But your finished bathroom will be so much more successful as a functional room if you have a sound understanding of the practicalities behind different elements of the design. Getting back to basics and questioning every choice you make ('What are the benefits of a big bath?', 'What exactly do I need to store?', 'Where would lights work best?') will ensure that a perfect balance between form and function is achieved.

bath

Generally, size will be the first consideration, closely followed by colour, material and shape (see 27–33). Be realistic about what will suit your bathroom. Even a modest-sized bath can be luxurious, fitted with whirlpool jets and with a power shower overhead (see 34).

shower

Do you know your water pressure and how your hot water is produced? Without these vital facts, you won't be able to choose the best shower for your needs (see 37). The style of the shower-head, the shape of the enclosure or the size of the tray are all secondary to the water flow (see 38–45).

basin

Where should I put my basin? How should I mount it? What kind of use will it get? These are the questions you should be asking yourself, in addition to exploring the benefits of ceramic versus glass, or stone troughs versus wooden bowls (see 46–52).

taps

Polished chrome or matt steel, old-fashioned brass or warm nickel? Whichever taps you choose, they should look good as well as being durable, and they need to be easy to use, too. Can you turn them with soapy hands, for example? (see 53–56)

wc

Not a glamorous subject, but one that deserves some thought. Think about comfort and hygiene, as well as design tricks like concealing the cistern or attaching the pan to the wall (see 13 and 58). You might even want to consider separating the toilet from the bathroom (60).

storage

If you use the bare minimum of toiletries and a few cleaning agents, you'll obviously need less storage than someone who revels in bottles galore and bales of towels. Make sure the furniture you choose – whether a medicine cabinet, display shelves or banks of fitted furniture – will be purposeful (see 62–67).

walls

How you finish your walls depends on personal taste and budget, from a quick slick of paint to painstaking tiling with tumbled marble mosaics (see 69–75). Don't be afraid to mix different surfaces so you get the waterproofing you need and the look you want (see 68).

floors

Beneath your feet, but not beneath your notice, a bathroom floor covering needs to be non-slip, comfortable for bare feet and, of course, waterproof (see 76). Compare the maintenance issues as well as the aesthetics of ceramic, stone, vinyl and wood (see 77–82).

lighting

Use light to decorate as much as to illuminate, with wall-washers, downlights and uplights creating mood and dimension in the bathroom. For practical purposes ensure there's sufficient light where it's really needed – by the mirror, for example (see 83–86).

heating

In the room where warmth matters most, heating is vital. If you want underfloor heating, you'll have to explore it at an early stage of the design, unless you want to re-lay your floor; and positioning of radiators is crucial (see 87–90).

getting inspiration

If you're bereft of creative ideas in terms of colour and style, or struggling to imagine a new layout, don't despair: sources of inspiration are all around you.

showrooms

Some showrooms offer row after uninspiring row of bathtubs, basins and taps, but the better ones will showcase their products in life-like displays. Within one showroom you may find 10 or 20 different bathroom looks, helping you imagine how your own completed bathroom could appear.

catalogues

Order a stack of bathroom catalogues via the Internet or by calling the hotline numbers on adverts. As well as technical information about a particular company's collections, there are pictures of the products in beautifully styled room-sets, which will allow you to see the potential of your own room.

magazines

Interior design magazines offer a 'through-the-keyhole' glimpse into other people's homes, helping you imagine what you can achieve with your own bathroom. Clip out the pictures you like and keep a file of useful names and numbers.

television

There is a plethora of home-decorating programmes on television showing the transformation of shabby rooms into splendid spaces. Featuring all stages of design, from gutting a room through to accessorising, they encourage you to see that dream designs can be realised. Expect your own renovation to take longer than 24 hours though!

other people's bathrooms

As well as taking careful note of friends' bathrooms, also pay attention to restrooms in restaurants and bars, as well as hotel bathrooms – you'll often see exciting design innovations used in commercial spaces.

likes and dislikes

One of the best – and easiest – ways to start planning a new bathroom is to think about how you use your old one. Stand in it with a pen and paper in hand and answer the following questions:

♥ **What's the best thing about the bathroom?**

✗ **What's the worst part of it?**

♥ **What looks good – but is impractical?**

✗ **What looks ugly – but is useful?**

♥ **Is there anything you don't want to change?**

You might think that the good natural light is the best thing; the small space is the worst; the polished chrome taps look good but show watermarks; the radiator looks terrible but is great for hanging towels; and you couldn't bear to change your large sash window. This gives you a starting point: you want to maximise space and make the most of the light from the window. You might want to consider matt chrome taps that won't show watermarks, and to change your radiator for an attractive design that will still provide hanging space.

Asking your partner – and even your children – for their opinions will help you create a plan of attack, and will highlight common likes and dislikes.

Another way to pinpoint your likes and dislikes is to create a folder of cuttings from magazines and brochures. Add in samples of tiles, paint colours and fabric swatches to show the textures, colours and materials you like. Similarly, create a folder of things you don't like – this is especially important if you are going to commission a designer to help you create your bathroom. They'll need to know what to avoid as much as what to include.

money matters

The often-raised question, 'how much does a new bathroom cost?' is as unanswerable as the age-old 'how long is a piece of string?' Innumerable factors influence the costs, with perhaps the most important being: how much are you prepared to spend?

five budgeting steps

1 • Set a budget: ask yourself how much you can afford and what a new bathroom is worth to you. Do you have any savings you can dip into or will you have to get a loan? Be realistic.

2 • Estimate costs: visit showrooms and look at price lists in catalogues. Add up the cost of every element in your design, and don't forget wall and floor finishes, taps, lighting and radiators. Add about 25% on to that total to pay for installation.

3 • Channelling the money: think about how best to apportion your pot of money. You could cut out installation costs by doing it yourself, but unless you're skilled, it could be a DIY disaster. Shop around for bargains: unbranded products usually cost less, and if you save on the basin and WC, you could spend more on a big and sturdy bathtub. Don't be tempted to skimp on 'moving parts' like taps and the shower though. Cheaper versions are more likely to break and may not be guaranteed.

4 • Schedule of payments: When will you have to pay? Designers may request a deposit in advance. On-site contractors may expect weekly payments. And some retailers may allow you to pay in instalments for their goods. Ensure your cash flow can cope with all demands.

5 • Contingency funds: Things go wrong, delays occur, and they always cost you money . . . you need to allow for the unexpected. Set aside 5–10% above your budget for any contingencies.

diy or not?

Some see DIY as a satisfying hobby or an exciting challenge; but to many others, it's a last resort. A tight budget is one of the main reasons for the hands-on approach to a renovation project, but whatever your motivation, are you prepared for the work?

If it's a question of simply re-painting walls to update a tired decor, any reasonably competent person can master it. Check out a DIY manual for advice on preparing walls beforehand, and get advice in the shop about the type of paint you're buying. Jobs such as plastering and tiling take a degree of expertise to complete them correctly, but with practice (and that trusty manual), you could succeed.

When it comes to plumbing and electrics though, it's best to step aside for the professionals. (In some cases, it's even illegal for a non-qualified person to undertake the work.)

Mistakes with pipes and wiring can not only be costly, but also dangerous, so save up the money – or put your pride aside – and get the experts involved.

where to start?

There are plenty of books to turn to, plus helpful websites and forums where like-minded beginners and enthusiasts are happy to answer specific queries. (Type 'bathroom design', a string of words, or even your specific query into a search engine.) Ask advice in the shop you buy the products from; the assistants may be knowledgeable or may have leaflets to help you. It's true that most products will come with their own set of instructions, but unless you're experienced, you'll probably find the technical guides practically incomprehensible.

6 bathroom designers

Designing a bathroom is easier than you may think: it's a matter of planning a layout, choosing the products to fit and deciding on a decorative scheme. There are so many sources of inspiration – and guides such as this book – that with some research and hard work, even an amateur can create a beautiful bathroom design.

However, the lay person really isn't qualified to tackle technical aspects, such as plumbing and electrics. Although your general contractor may be able to advise you on these areas, you could choose to put the whole design in the hands of an expert rather than do it yourself.

five types of designer

1 • Architect: trained in structural design, most will usually take on only major works, such as the design or re-modelling of a whole house.

2 • Interior architect: combines structural expertise with an interior design service

3 • Interior designer: focuses on the inside of a home, rather than the external structure. May be able to tackle straightforward structural changes.

4 • Interior decorator: offers a service of 'superficial' decorating, rather than technical or structural alterations

5 • Bathroom designer: employed by a bathroom showroom, a bathroom designer demonstrates how the retailer's products can be used to create a dream bathroom. Some may be solely design-led, whereas others may be more sales-led, so be sure you understand their motivation.

who does what?

Be sure you decide with your designer where responsibility lies. Who will manage the project? Who will choose and hire the contractors? Who will be in charge of final decoration? There are many different levels of design service, so check exactly what you will be paying for. Make sure there's a contract and that you fully understand it.

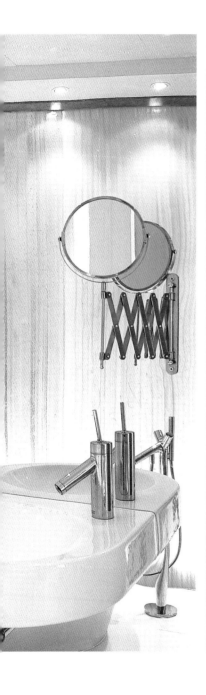

bathroom contractors

7

Unless you're an expert at DIY and have the relevant qualifications to do all the work yourself, you'll be calling on the services of professionals to help you complete your bathroom project.

Just think of all the different elements in a bathroom. You (or your designer) may need to hire a whole team of workers, including a plumber, plasterer, tiler, electrician, builder and painter. But often you'll just hire one person, a general contractor. He (or she) will be capable of the rough work, and even the more specialist jobs like plastering or tiling, but may sub-contract the plumbing and electrical jobs to other professionals. This will save you the responsibility of doing more hiring, and your main contractor will oversee their work and pay them for it.

Of course, finding a reliable and talented contractor is never easy. You'll hear plenty of horror stories about slipshod cowboys and dishonest traders. Picking a name at random out of a directory is a real lottery, so to give yourself the best chance of hitting the jackpot:

• Ask friends and neighbours for recommendations

• Get estimates from at least three tradespeople

• Make sure that your contractor is a member of the relevant guild and is properly qualified

• Ask any potential contractors for references – and make sure that you check them

• Make sure your contractor carries insurance – for personal injury, for injury the work may cause to others and for damage to goods or property

• Get a written contract which includes a schedule of payments (with a 5% fee to be held back until you're satisfied with the work) and penalty clauses in case of late completion

• Check whether the work will be guaranteed or not

plumbing

Water supply and drainage, taps and showers, water-based heating systems – these are all the remit of the plumber. This specialist tradesperson is invaluable in bathroom installations, not least because he or she can bring practical experience to the project, as well as technical know-how.

what a plumber can do for you

• Rough plumbing: investigating and upgrading the below-floor or wall-buried pipework; installing pipes to fit the layout of the new bathroom

• Water pressure: measuring your water pressure, so you know what taps and shower will be suitable; boosting the water pressure if necessary

• Heating: calculating what size radiator is needed to warm the bathroom; advising on (and installing) the best boiler for your general heating and hot-water needs

• Installation: of the bathroom suite and the brassware (in other words, the taps and shower), connecting the hot and cold feeds to the brassware, and connecting the drainage pipes to the wastes

• Specifying: buying basic bathroom fittings and fixtures at reduced prices from trade suppliers

Make sure you check your plumber is fully qualified for all aspects of the work (including installing a gas boiler, for example). Different aspects of plumbing are governed by health and safety or building regulations, particularly regarding water supply and sanitation, and you need to be assured that these are being correctly followed.

9 the boiler

Conventional boilers, back boilers, condensing boilers, combination boilers . . . all produce hot water (and heat your home) in different ways. Some systems store hot and cold water in tanks and feed them to your plumbing outlets by gravity or by pump; others create hot water instantaneously on demand; and still others combine both methods.

It's important you understand what type of system you have so you can make decisions regarding the products you'll install in your bathroom. For example, there's no point fitting a big bath if your hot-water cylinder can't supply sufficient hot water to fill it. And if you want to be able to run two showers at the same time, you'll need to have a high-pressure, high-capacity system.

Ask your plumber for advice on what your current system is capable of and consider whether you need to change or upgrade your system to achieve your dream bathroom.

10 electrics – and water

Water and electricity are a dangerous mix, which is why there are so many regulations governing such matters as the use of electrical appliances, voltage limits and types of electrical outlets permitted in wet areas. However, regulations vary greatly between countries, from the types of switches and sockets allowed (if at all) in the room to the qualifications needed (if any) before someone can tackle electrical work in bathrooms.

what an electrician can do for you

• Lighting: your electrician should be able to advise on the types of light fittings you need, such as waterproof, water-resistant or low-voltage, and will wire up the system safely
• Switches and sockets: ask for guidance on the positioning of sockets and switches. Let him know exactly what you wish to use the sockets for: shaver, toothbrush, hairdryer etc, so he can ensure they meet all safety requirements.
• Electrically operated plumbing: pump systems (for supplying or draining water) work by electricity, and also water is heated electrically in some showers and boilers. Your plumber may be trained to complete the installation otherwise it's best to turn to an electrician.
• Ventilation: it's essential – and in some countries, if the bathroom doesn't have a window, it's a legal requirement. Ducted systems suck steam and odours outside, keeping the air fresh and reducing moisture in the bathroom. Ventilation often works in conjunction with the lighting, activated when the light is switched on, but running for a further 15–20 minutes after the light is extinguished.

best-laid plans

11

Whether you're doing everything yourself or calling in contractors, you'll need plans to refer to during the refurbishment. Mistakes occur when ideas are left vague, so creating a drawing will ensure the re-design is kept on track.

floor-plan

• Make yourself a rough pencil sketch of the shape of the room, as seen with a bird's-eye view.

• Measure and mark down the length of every wall, and section of wall. Also measure the height of the room and note this alongside the sketch.

• Measure the width and height of windows and doors and note where they start and finish. Mark those on the drawing too. Add details such as the swing of the door.

• Mark plumbing outlets such as the soil pipe, and any major or permanent fixtures such as a boiler, or any housing for gas pipes.

• Now transfer this rough sketch to a piece of graph paper and draw it accurately to scale.

You could also sketch each elevation (i.e., what a wall looks like as you face it) to show heights, but the basic bird's-eye view floor plan is normally enough to design a layout.

layout

Take careful note of the measurements of the bath, WC, basin, furniture and other fixtures you want to include in your bathroom. Draw them to the same scale as the floor plan and cut them out. Now position them on your plan to see what will fit and make sure you consider circulation space around each piece, as well as the height they reach.

mood boards

To help you decide on the look you want (or to help your interior designer know your tastes), collect samples of tiles, paint charts, fabric swatches and lots of cuttings from magazines and brochures. Glue them in place on cardboard to give a visual overview of the general 'mood' you want in your finished bathroom.

structural alterations 12

With your floor plan in front of you, strewn with cut-out pieces of paper that you're trying to arrange into a sensible layout, you may despair of the size or shape of the bathroom. And standing in a dark and dingy space, with a low, oppressive ceiling and awkwardly positioned fixtures, you may think it can never be a light and welcoming room.

It is possible to alter the shell of the room and to change the structure to your advantage. But are you prepared for extra expense and upheaval? Bear in mind too, there may be delays while you wait for permission to make the changes (in some cases, structural alterations are governed by local laws and regulations and you need approval before you can start – check with your designer, contractor or local planning office).

three good reasons for structural alterations

1 to create more physical space

Demolishing walls to borrow space from a neighbouring room and removing bulky obstacles such as cupboards will enlarge the bathroom, giving you more room to fit in everything you want.

2 to enhance the sense of space

Raising or lowering a ceiling or floor, re-sizing windows or adding a skylight are all ways of improving the space you've got. Concealing pipes, bringing in more natural light and creating better proportions will do wonders for a small bathroom as well (see 13).

3 to increase the flexibility of design

Strengthening the walls allows you to wall-mount fittings, while strengthening the floor means the joists can support a cast-iron tub. Simply by re-positioning the boiler or the soil pipe, moving the door or even changing the way it swings, you open up new layout possibilities.

bijou bathrooms 13

If allowed to change only one thing about their bathroom, most people would ask for a bigger space. But unfortunately, as it's not always possible to wave a magic wand and make the walls move outwards, the majority learn to live with the tight dimensions of the room.

All is not lost though, for with careful planning and judicious selection of fittings and fixtures, you can create a small bathroom that displays fine aesthetics, maximises every inch of space and even fools the eye into thinking the closed-in walls are not so close after all.

five solutions for small bathrooms

1 • Cutting it fine: having realised that small bathrooms are a big problem, many companies are now offering space-saving solutions. Look for shortened or tapered bathtubs, short-projection basins and off-set WCs, as well as reduced-depth cabinets.

2 • Hanging it all: the eye looks at the floor space and judges the size of the room accordingly, so if you mount your basin, WC (see 58) and furniture on the wall, you'll immediately create the impression of more space in the room.

3 • Doubling up: fit two items into one space – for example, a bath-shower combination, furniture that doubles as a basin support, or a laundry basket that's also a seat.

4 • On reflection: mirrors are an excellent means of visually expanding a space. A wall-to-wall mirror will appear to double the size of the room and even a small mirror can be positioned to bounce light around the bathroom.

5 • Pale and interesting: choose light colours to make surfaces recede, such as white-tiled walls, beige stone flooring and translucent green glass screens.

big bathrooms 14

In some ways, big bathrooms are as hard to design as small ones. The more flexibility you have, the more difficult it can be.

three common mistakes in designing big bathrooms

1 • Wall-hugging: in small bathrooms, most products will butt up against walls. In big bathrooms they don't have to – and in fact, it looks wrong if all the fixtures seem to shrink away from the centre of the room and hug the perimeter.

2 • Overloading: you may have room for a WC, bidet, two-person bath, steam cabin, twin basins, bank of furniture – but you don't have to have it all. There's no formula for the perfect bathroom, so only choose those pieces you will actually use.

3 • Over-styling: don't think that big has to mean grand. You can keep your bathroom simple without it seeming empty, and you don't have to fill it with paraphernalia or make it look too busy.

three good ideas for big bathrooms

1 • Focusing: consider using a big, freestanding bath as a focal point in the room. It doesn't have to be slap-bang in the middle: use it to draw your eye through the room or towards one corner.

2 • Zoning: use partitions, changes in floor height and different colours/materials to define zones: for example, hide the WC and bidet behind a glass-brick wall, and separate wet areas from dry areas with different floor coverings.

3 • Expanding: don't expand the area, but expand the use of the bathroom. Can you use a section as a walk-in wardrobe, or create a comfortable sitting area in one corner where you can pamper yourself?

en-suite bathrooms

Adjacent to the bedroom, the en-suite bathroom has a very specialised and personal nature. As well as thinking about the generalities encountered in any bathroom renovation, give thought to the design issues that are peculiar to the en-suite.

• Free flowing: whereas a family bathroom opens off a corridor, an en suite is an extension of a bedroom. For that reason, design coherence between the two rooms, such as a similar colour scheme, textures or materials in both, is very important.

• Personal taste: casual visitors won't usually see your en-suite bathroom. This means that you can really make it a design to please you – not a showpiece for guests. View it as a chance to explore your own ideas and experiment a little with design.

• Privacy: how open or how private your en suite is depends on you (and the person you may share the bedroom with). If you don't close the door, do you even need one?

finding the space

Creating an en-suite bathroom where none exists isn't always simple, but it's worth the effort for the convenience it brings. It's also likely to raise the saleability of your property as an en suite is often rated a necessity, rather than a luxury. Here are three ways you might find the space:

1 • Borrowing: if there's space to spare in the room next door, consider borrowing some (or all) of it for your new en suite.

2 • Partitioning: if your bedroom is large enough, you can partition off a section of the room to create a bathroom.

3 • Adapting: even a cupboard, a corridor or a landing can be` turned into a shower room, with some clever design work and professional help.

open-plan bathrooms

A relatively new trend, but one that's attracting growing interest, is the open-plan bathroom. A bolder, braver version of the en suite, this is a bathroom within a bedroom – with no walls for privacy. Its extremely open nature means it's not suitable for all lifestyles and tastes, so it may be worth building flexibility into the design, allowing it to be 'walled away' if your situation changes.

three practical aspects to consider

1 • Disturbance: if you share your bedroom with a partner, make sure you're both on the same timetable. If one gets up earlier or goes to bed later than the other, the person sleeping will be disturbed by the noise of water running, by lights being switched on and by general bustle in the open-plan bathroom.

2 • Privacy: in a family house, you may want to put a lock on the bedroom door so you can bathe and use the toilet without fear of interruption. And on the subject of the WC, no matter how close you are to your partner, there are probably some things you just don't want to share! So consider tucking the loo behind a screen or create a separate cloakroom to house it.

3 • Ventilation: there's a lot of fabric in a bedroom – curtains, bedlinen, and often carpet too. Unless you want to risk your clothes getting damp or your carpet growing mouldy, good ventilation is essential to whisk steam away before it condenses.

the family bathroom

The typical family bathroom has multiple roles to play: a fun-filled water-park for young kids, a beauty parlour or grooming zone for teenagers, a quiet retreat for mum or dad . . . Its main purpose is, of course, to house essential washing facilities (bath, shower and basin) – and also a toilet if there's no separate cloakroom.

As the family bathroom is used by a variety of people ranging in age and size, with different needs and tastes, the design shouldn't be too radical, or geared too much towards either adults or children. Make moderation, practicality and flexibility your watchwords.

moderation

- Standard sanitaryware in white or cream is inoffensive and will stand the test of time.

- If basins and toilets are too high the children will struggle to reach them, if they're too low you'll have to stoop uncomfortably.

practicality

- With kids around, things are sure to get dropped and spilt, and water will certainly be splashed about, so make sure your floor and wall coverings can cope.

- It's amazing how much grime teenagers bring into the house – have you seen a bath after a football game? Quick-clean surfaces will make life much easier.

flexibility

- If toys for children's bathtime clutter the room, make sure there's plenty of storage where you can bundle them away before your relaxing soak in the tub. You want to be able to switch from mayhem to calm with minimum effort.

- Queues outside a family bathroom in the morning are the norm. Consider creating a separate cloakroom, or providing a basin in a teenager's bedroom, to decrease the strain on the family bathroom.

18

the children's bathroom

If your child is lucky enough to have a dedicated bathroom, you can decorate it with kids-only in mind. But even so, remember that little ones don't stay little – allow some leeway for the bathroom to adapt as children grow up.

three essential elements of children's bathrooms

1 practicality

- Set the WC and basin low (or with a small step in front) so children can reach in easily.
- Set the bath into a plinth so the sides are low enough for little ones to climb in and out.
- Make sure all surfaces are waterproof, and durable enough to withstand any hard knocks.

2 fun

- Kids love colour, so wave goodbye to any thoughts of neutrals. Consider bright waterproof paint, a border of tiles in zesty shades or even colourful stickers to jazz up plain white tiles or sanitaryware.
- Buy a toy chest that doubles as a seat, use decorated or shaped mirrors that are angled downwards, and add fun doorknobs, drawer handles and clothes hooks.
- Create a theme around a cartoon character, using lots of accessories and logos to set the scene

3 safety

- Hot water is the biggest danger to children in bathrooms, so make sure the taps and shower have anti-scald devices and thermostatic mixers are set to low temperatures.
- There's sure to be water splashed around, so choose a non-slip, soft-underfoot floor covering, like textured cork or cushioned vinyl. Add a rubber bathmat so children don't slip in the tub.
- Make sure there's no lock on the door so children can't get locked in.

the personal sanctuary

If you need a place to rest and unwind, a retreat from the demands of everyday living, establish the bathroom as your private sanctuary. No longer simply a room for cleansing the body, the bathroom can also detoxify the mind.

A personal sanctuary is as individual as its creator. For some, deep-pile towels, hydro-massage showers and a wealth of expensive scrubs and soaps are essential. Others prefer a more ascetic, pared-down experience. But whether you opt for high-maintenance heaven or the simplest haven, there are three things you can't do without:

1 • A comfortable bathtub: it doesn't have to be vast in size or boast whirlpool jets – all you need is a tub that will cradle your body as you lie back and relax.

2 • Adjustable lighting: if you have lights on dimmers, you can turn them down to a comfortable glow. Failing that, switch off all the lights and bathe by candlelight.

3 • A lock on the door: make sure you can't be interrupted as you soak away your stress!

the home spa

Even without a masseuse to hand, you can turn your bathroom into a private spa. Be inspired by luxury health clubs to create a hydrozone that will invigorate or relax, as your mood takes you.

Whirlpool or spa baths, steam cabins and multi-jet power showers all offer a range of multi-sensory therapeutic benefits. These include:

• Hydro-massage: varying spray patterns, pulses of water and bubbling air have a range of positive effects, including improving circulation, relaxing muscles and easing joints
• Chromotherapy: top-of-the-range baths and shower cabins boast light therapy, creating positive psychological effects with coloured lighting (for example, red to stimulate, yellow for happiness, orange to revitalise and green for relaxation)
• Aromatherapy: some steam cabins include infusers to waft the scent of aromatic oils or herbs into the cabin (otherwise you can add essential oils to a burner by the side of the bath)

the wet room

A wet room – a bathroom with a shower but no shower tray – is at the cutting edge of bathroom design. The water from the shower cascades on to the floor, where a drainage system channels it away. Often, the water is allowed to splash freely as there's no shower enclosure, however, in some cases, a screen or wall is erected to protect other areas of the bathroom.

Although a wet room looks simple, creating a leak-proof room is very complex. Firstly, the whole structure of the room must be stable: wooden joists may need to be stabilised so they don't flex. For this reason, wet rooms suit the ground floor or basement, rather than an upper floor. The entire room will need to be tanked (waterproofed), usually with a layer of bitumen, fibreglass or lead. On top of this is laid the watertight floor- and wall-covering, such as stone or ceramic tiles, and the grout must be totally waterproof – an epoxy-resin mixture, for example.

spray on

The showering system in your wet room could be a ceiling-mounted rose, a wall-mounted handset or even a multi-jet shower panel. And if you have enough space, you can position the shower away from the wall and install a freestanding central column.

your style dare you defy definition? 22

You might not have actually put a name to the style you prefer, or you may not think your taste can be neatly pigeonholed into a particular category, but it's likely that your bathroom will veer towards one of the following five styles.

1 clinical

Imagine a laboratory-like space: hygienic, wipe-clean surfaces in stainless steel, polished chrome and high-gloss white acrylic, expanses of white tiles, accents of frosty green glass, streamlined storage. Although somewhat cold and hard in appearance, the clinical bathroom is a minimalist's heaven.

2 organic

A back-to-nature feel, where glaring white is banished in favour of soft cream. Wood and stone, with prominent grain and rough texture, are an integral part of the design, whether in the form of a feature basin, flooring or accessories. Tiles in neutral colours and with pitted surfaces carry a raw feel. Add a jungle of plants for bathroom wilderness.

3 classic

Elegantly traditional: gold-coloured taps with ceramic handles and flared spouts, decorative tiles in deeper tones, a roll-top bath with claw feet. A dark wood vanity unit with a Carrara marble basin surround adds rich appeal. The window is dressed with fabric drapes.

4 colourful

The bolder, the better: if you're brave enough, choose a coloured suite and team it with complementary shades of paint on the walls and bright lino flooring. Or opt for plain white sanitaryware and choose a single accent colour, going crazy with bright mosaic tiles, rich fluffy towels and patterned roller blinds.

5 eclectic

A mix-and-match approach, in which the traditional is confidently combined with the contemporary and the bold and bright are placed alongside naturals and neutrals. Styled with flair, it doesn't look haphazard, but is balanced to create a warm and user-friendly bathroom.

contemporary 23

The word minimalist is much over-used in describing clean-lined, contemporary homes, but few really embrace the absolute spirit of minimalism. The in-vogue bathroom is more likely to follow a path of comfortable minimalism that balances simplicity and pared-down lines with the practicalities of everyday family life.

five typical materials

1 • Glass: acid-etched or sand-blasted, frosted glass has an attractive icy appearance. Tinged with green, blue or grey, a gentle hint of colour is added to the design.

2 • Ceramic: white ceramic sanitaryware follows strictly simple geometry (squares and circles are both popular), while white ceramic tiles, in brick-shapes or squares, offer subtle texture for interest. Ceramic mosaics in watery colours are often used for shower areas.

3 • Stone: slate flooring brings a rougher, organic feel underfoot; expanses of pale, honed limestone denote simplicity.

4 • Metal: shower controls and taps are plated in silvery chrome, stainless steel or aluminium and the same polished or matt metals are used as accents elsewhere.

5 • Wood: basins, shelves and accessories in tropical hardwoods such as wenge or iroko (preferably from sustainable resources) or in fashionable plywood are teamed with harder materials for interesting contrast.

five typical products

1 • Baths and showers: high-tech spa products include steam cabins, whirlpool baths and hydro-massage showers

2 • WC: wall-mounted WC, with the cistern concealed and a discreet push-button flush

3 • Radiator: ladder radiators and towel-rails, wall-hung to conserve space

4 • Furniture: simple vanity unit in chunky wood, often just a shelf cantilevered from the wall, with double basins inset or mounted on top

5 • Brassware: single-lever mixer taps, wall-mounted in order to conceal all the pipework

traditional

Typically Edwardian, Victorian or Art Deco in style, the traditionally styled bathroom exudes comfort and warmth. Colours are deeper, materials softer (even fabric makes an appearance), and decorative details offer no purpose other than to please the eye.

five typical materials

1 • Glass: traditional glass tends to be crystal clear or etched with patterns for both decoration and privacy.

2 • Ceramic: sanitaryware is off-white and is moulded with rims, lips and decorative plinths. Tiles are coloured in deep, glossy hues or printed with border designs and other motifs.

3 • Stone: marble and speckled granite add robust and classical notes to the room; not only used on walls and floors, but also for bath and basin surrounds.

4 • Metal: shower and taps are plated in warm, burnished metals, such as brass, or brass alloyed with nickel or pewter.

5 • Wood: furniture is finished with rich mahogany and cherry wood veneers and elaborate carving adds an opulent note

five typical products

1 • Baths and showers: enamelled, cast-iron roll-top baths, the exterior painted in chalky shades, perch on claw-foot legs; the shower features a ceramic handle and skirted rose

2 • WC: the wooden-seated WC stands like an elegant throne, with a visible cistern and pull-chain flush

3 • Radiator: a cast-iron column radiator in pewter or painted finish stands underneath the window

4 • Furniture: deep floor-standing vanity units with moulded panels and marble tops hold inset oval basins

5 • Brassware: deck-mounted pillar taps and bridge mixers display fluted spouts and chunky crosshead handles or ceramic levers

project management

Any project, whether it's a bathroom renovation or a business endeavour, needs a manager. This person has an overview of the whole work, is a central point of contact for all involved, and really understands 'the big picture'. The manager can be hands-on, or can choose to delegate tasks appropriately and check results to ensure that the jobs have been completed to satisfaction. He or she bears ultimate responsibility for the success of the project.

should I project manage?

You need to decide whether you will be project manager on your own bathroom refurbishment. Be realistic:

• Do you have the time? If it's a major job, you'll need to be around to oversee the work or be there to deal with problems when they crop up.

• Do you have the skills? You'll need to liaise with the professional builders, tilers, plumbers, etc – can you explain to them what you need them to do?

• Can you afford to hire anyone else? Although it's unlikely you'll be hiring someone who is simply a project manager (unless you're building or revamping a whole house), you could put the responsibility of project management on your interior designer, architect or even on a general contractor who is carrying out the renovation work.

project management involves controlling

• Costs: keep the project on budget by ensuring the right products – and the correct amounts – are bought. If the unexpected occurs, be prepared to use some of your contingency fund, but see if there's another solution apart from pouring money in.

• Schedule: ensure not only that work is completed on time, but that all the products arrive on time – this is basic supply-chain management. You have to make sure that the tiles you ordered 4 weeks ago will arrive when your tiler needs them.

• Quality: check the work as each stage is being completed. Look at the pipes before they've covered over; check the finish on the plastered walls. Make sure you're happy with one job before another begins.

step-by-step

Your head may be spinning with ideas: you're unsure where to start or how to structure the renovation project. It helps to make a list of everything you have to do and then draft a time-line, so you know your priorities.

ten-point checklist

1 • Begin your research: get inspiration from showrooms and catalogues. Ask lots of questions, visit web forums, read articles. You can spend months doing this while you save up your money.

2 • Make lists: note your likes and dislikes, what you want to include (or avoid) in your new bathroom; make a wish-list of your dream items.

3 • Set a budget: consider how much money you're willing to spend on the bathroom; whittle your wish-list down to your 'must-haves' and start collecting information on prices of products; get labour estimates from possible contractors.

4 • Select a contractor or contractors: having negotiated fees and checked references, have in-depth discussions with your chosen contractor about availability, time schedule and responsibilities.

5 • Draw up plans: sketch a floor plan to scale and make a final decision about the products that you want. Involve your contractor in the technical aspects.

6 • Order products: order all the tiles, taps, bath, basin etc and check if other materials are needed (e.g., will your tiler supply the grout?). Find out the lead times for each product (bearing in mind that in Europe some factories shut for a month in the summer).

7 • Sign a contract: now that you and your contractor know the timings, the exact products and every detail, negotiate a final fee and agree a contract.

8 • Start renovating: your contractor (or you) can now commence the operation by gutting the original bathroom.

9 • Oversee the project: even if you're not project managing, it's worth popping your head into the bathroom occasionally to see how work is progressing. Aim to avert problems before they happen or solve them as they arise.

10 • Final details: check the bathroom thoroughly, both with your contractor and alone. Present the contractor with a snagging list (e.g., straighten shelf, replace chipped tiles, etc) and don't pay the retained portion of the fee until your bathroom is totally finished and you are completely happy with it.

2

part two

getting down to the detail

it's bathtime

The bath is usually the single largest element of a bathroom and its size alone makes it a focal point. But add good looks, design innovation and ergonomic styling to its monolithic bulk and you'll have a centrepiece you can be proud of.

testing, testing

Don't be embarrassed about climbing into the tub in the showroom and sitting up and lying back in it. Does it offer good support for your neck, back and arms? Is it both long enough and wide enough? Above all, is it comfortable?

inside out

As well as actually testing the bath to check its comfort, make a point of looking at the specifications in the brochure, which detail the internal dimensions as well as external ones. Compare different models and, strangely, you may find that some 170cm-long baths have more room inside than 180cm-long models.

the impact of colour

For the past few years, simple white has been the favoured colour choice for tubs. Now, however, focal point baths come in all shades, from bright -hued composites to translucent glass. Don't be frightened of opting for colour, but temper it with white sanitaryware.

twice as nice

Shared bathing won't be romantic and relaxing unless it's comfortable. Look for a double-ended bath that slopes gently at both ends (you can both lean back), with a central waste (so no one sits on the plug!), and no pre-drilled tap holes at one end (you can install taps centrally).

outsiders

With the exception of certain tubs like roll-tops, most baths require aprons or panels to give them a finished appearance. Consider how your bath will look when installed. Do you want to box it in and tile the surround, or add acrylic side and end panels to match? You can even find stylish patterned glass or metal vanity surrounds.

28
material matters

Glass, wood, stone and even stainless steel baths are now available, but the three most common materials are acrylic, cast-iron and pressed steel.

acrylic

Available in numerous colours (though white is the current trend), acrylic also gives the greatest variety in terms of shape and size. Look for acrylic composites, which are stronger and won't flex so much, and double-skinned acrylics for greater heat insulation.

advantages
- Can be moulded into complex shapes
- Lightweight
- Super-smooth and non-porous
- Warm to the touch
- Won't chip

disadvantages
- Cheaper acrylics are flimsy and will flex
- Needs strengthening with glass fibre or wooden supports
- Thin acrylics aren't very heat insulating
- May scratch and stain

cast-iron

Traditionally used for roll-top baths, cast-iron baths come with a vitreous enamel interior and the exterior comes ready-painted, or primed for your own colour choice. Look at the beautiful uneven surface of the enamel glaze inside a cast-iron tub: it suggests a unique and timeless beauty that more modern materials can't capture.

advantages
- Excellent heat insulation (once the material has warmed up)
- Durable and stable
- Exterior can be colour-matched to your decor
- Scratch-resistant

disadvantages
- Extremely heavy
- Limited in shape and size due to weight and rigidity
- Enamel may chip

pressed steel

For the best of both worlds, look at enamelled pressed steel: it's an excellent compromise between the lightweight malleability of acrylic and the solidity of cast-iron. Look for baths with thicker layers of steel for greater strength and better heat insulation.

advantages
- Relatively strong and durable
- Good choice of shapes
- Scratch-resistant
- Lightweight
- Cost-effective

disadvantages
- Thinner layers of steel are not very heat-insulating
- Enamel may chip

shapes

It's important to consider both the external and internal shape of a bath. The external shape will have an impact on where you locate the tub in your bathroom and what you can place alongside it, while the internal shape will have more bearing on your comfort, and how easy (or difficult) it will be to clean the bath.

rectangle

The straight sides and right angles of the boxy shape enable the bath to be positioned flush with a wall or tight into a corner, while the rounded internal angles cradle the body better and are easy to clean.

oval

An oval exterior is usually found on a freestanding tub, such as a roll-top, which is ideal for central placement in the bathroom. The soft angles and the rounded interior make it comfortable to sit or lie in.

round

Although the external shape is smooth and ergonomic, circular tubs are bulky and demand a big bathroom. The internal shape makes it easier to sit up than to lie down, unless it's moulded to hold one or two bodies.

corner

Quadrant-shaped corner baths present a soft curve to the room, but do take up a lot of space. The internal shape is sometimes a little awkward, so look for models specially contoured to the body.

offset or tapered

An offset corner tub or tapered rectangle give the benefits of those common shapes, but in a more space-saving form.

small and snug

Although an average rectangular bathtub measures only 170 x 75cm, if your bathroom suffers from space restrictions, even this standard size can be problematical.

- Length: Several manufacturers offer space-saving baths only 150 or 160cm long, and sit-up tubs measure only 110–140cm in length.
- Width: Look for baths that are 65 or 70cm wide, but bear in mind the tight internal dimensions of 50cm or less.

To ensure your bathing experience in a small bathtub is as comfortable as possible, look for tapered or offset styles (the narrower end will be the foot end), deep tubs (if you can't lie flat at least the water will still cover you) and straight internal sides (you lose a lot of space if the bath slopes inwards).

the bigger, the better?

If you're blessed with a large bathroom, surely it makes sense to fill the space with a capacious bath? But before you take the plunge and opt for a 2m-long monolith, weigh the potential drawbacks against the obvious luxurious benefits.

how long will it take to fill the bath?

Depending on the water pressure (and the flow rate your bath tap allows), it could take 15 minutes or more to fill the bath to a reasonable level.

how much hot water?

If you have a storage boiler, check the hot water storage capacity. You may find your tank runs dry before your bath is even half full.

how much will it cost?

This consideration is not just the cost of the bath itself (though big baths do tend to be pricey), but the amount of water it uses, and the amount of energy needed to heat that water. It's not the most environmentally friendly, or cost-conscious, option.

modern baths

Sleek lines and architectural geometry distinguish the contemporary tub. But that's where the generalisations end. It can't be categorised by a single material, colour, style or size. And on-going product development and technological advances have allowed the modern bathtub to break free of its past limitations.

big and boxy

Defined by high straight sides and sharp angles, these freestanding giants are made possible because of the strength and stability of composite materials that mix stone with resin, or even acrylic with more robust components.

pillow talk

As well as interiors contoured to cocoon your body, you'll find integrated bath pillows or removable back rests. Many contemporary baths are designed to offer a high degree of internal comfort.

bottoms up

A modern variation on the roll-top sees this oval tub raised off the ground on a wooden platform or plinth or in a tubular steel cradle. The added height and mix of materials adds a new dimension to the design.

sailing away

Boat-building technology comes into play in the construction of waterproof tubs made from tropical hardwoods (see 23) or marine ply. They require maintenance to remain watertight, but are worth it for the stunning organic centrepiece they create.

filling station

Taps are the usual means of filling a bath. However, a neat contemporary option is a bath filler actually inside the tub, commonly integrated into the overflow. It delivers a strong stream of water to quickly fill the bath and takes away the problem of where to site the taps.

33 traditional baths

With its classical elegance, the roll-top bath continues to hold its place at the heart of the traditional bathroom, and in recent years, has been borrowed by the modernists to form a centrepiece in the contemporary bathroom too.

three types of roll-top bath

1 • Original: with ornate claw feet, enamelled interior and painted exterior. You can get these cast-iron antiques from salvage yards and specialist dealers.

2 • Reproduction: identical in style to the original, these are newly manufactured and readily available. Some use lighter materials, such as acrylic composites (see 28).

3 • Updated: drawing on the lines of the classic roll-top, the modern version substitutes the claw feet with tubular steel legs, or even a plinth (see 32).

Some roll-tops have a squared-off end so the tub can be placed against a wall or in a corner, but most are oval-shaped freestanding pieces. This means that the waste pipe and hot- and cold-water feeds will be visible where they exit and enter the bath. The pipes to the bath will need to run below the floor, and some structural work may be required, depending on the joists and subfloor. You may even need to raise the height of the floor or create a platform for the bath to stand on (see 12).

Other traditional bath forms are the slipper style and the bateau tub. A slipper bath has one end raised higher than the other, forming a shape that resembles an arched shoe – hence its name. The bateau takes its title from the French for boat, and is a high-sided, flat-bottomed tub, often in burnished, hand-beaten copper.

34

spa and whirlpool baths time to pamper yourself

Whirlpool and spa baths are the ultimate luxury in the bathroom, creating a private pampering zone where you can sink into bubbling water, blissfully while away the hours and wave away your bodily aches (see 19 and 20).

same difference?

The terms spa and whirlpool are sometimes used synonymously, but the two methods of hydro-massage are actually very different.

• Spa bath: Holes in the base of the bath bubble air upwards for a soft, fizzy feeling. Spa baths commonly have 150–200 microjets for complete body coverage.

• Whirlpool bath: Water is sucked inwards and injected back into the bath with force. It's a much stronger effect than a spa, and it's usual to have only 6–12 jets, positioned around the sides of the bath to target specific areas such as neck, back and feet.

• Spa-whirlpool combos: Some baths combine spa jets with whirlpool jets for a dual-action massage. They can be used simultaneously or independently.

medical miracles?

The health benefits of hydro-massage are widely recognised: improved blood circulation, stimulated lymphatic drainage, increased oxygenation to the skin, and relaxed muscles. It's ideal if you're feeling tense and aching, and is also believed to help lessen the pain of arthritis and rheumatism. The soothing psychological effects of a relaxing massage should not be underestimated either.

stay safe and sound

Hygiene is a vital consideration with home spa systems. Stagnant water lingering in the pipework can be a breeding ground for bacteria. Look for the following features:

• Inclined pipes: these will facilitate water drainage

• Closed jets: if the bath is in use without the whirlpool, the jets are sealed to prevent soap and sediment entering

• Air drying: warm air is blown through the pipes after use to ensure they are totally dry

• Disinfection system: cleaning fluids are released into the pipes to ensure bacteria can't linger

• UV light system: this sanitises the pipes by destroying bacteria

careful!

With regard to safety, look for jets that have an automatic cut-off should they become blocked (for example, by your hair). Bear in mind too that low-voltage electricity is involved, as both the pump and touch-button controls are electrically operated. Always ask a qualified professional to install whatever system you choose.

comfort zone

Your massage bath needs to be a totally relaxing experience, so look for a comfortable internal shape, including arm rests, foot rests and soft head and neck cushions. Also, consider noise levels: if the system is too loud, you won't be able to relax. Ask to hear a model tested in the showroom, or choose a brand that boasts whisper-quiet operation.

extra features

The top models are packed with extra features including integrated radios and CD players, soothing soundtracks (rainforest effects, for example), underwater lights, chromotherapy settings and even ultrasound massage.

grand plans or small spaces

If your immediate thought is that you can't fit a spa or whirlpool tub into your modest-sized bathroom, don't despair. They really do come in all shapes and sizes. From large corner models or freestanding round tubs for 2 or more people to shorter, narrow, sit-up tubs for small bathrooms.

over-bath showers

If you lack the space for a shower enclosure in addition to a bath, an over-bath shower offers an ideal solution. And even if your bathroom does boast a separate shower cubicle, a secondary shower above the bath will be useful for rinsing off soap, and to save you dashing – dripping wet – across the room to the shower.

You can create your own over-bath shower very simply, with a standard bathtub. A basic shower-mixer tap can be retrofitted with surprising ease, but if you are totally renovating the bathroom, then plan for a fixed showerhead above, or a wall-mounted shower attachment on a slider rail.

Some companies offer tubs specifically designed for over-bath showers. They are modified to allow for more comfortable showering and offer a variety of useful benefits.

space to manoeuvre

Special bath-shower tubs bulge outwards at one end, to create a circular or square area that acts as a generous showering space. You may have as much as 20cm extra elbow room at the showering end.

grip, not slip

Specialist baths incorporate a textured surface at the showering end to give your feet some traction, so you don't have to use a rubber mat to stop yourself slipping.

screening programme

Tubs with a rounded showering end come with their own custom-fitted, curved glass screens to keep splashes inside. If you are simply modifying a standard straight-sided tub though, it won't be a problem to fit a straight glass panel (see 36).

obstacle course

Do think about where you are positioning bath taps, soap dishes and storage racks in relation to the showering area. You don't want them where you'll bang your knees and elbows – but you will want your toiletries within easy reach.

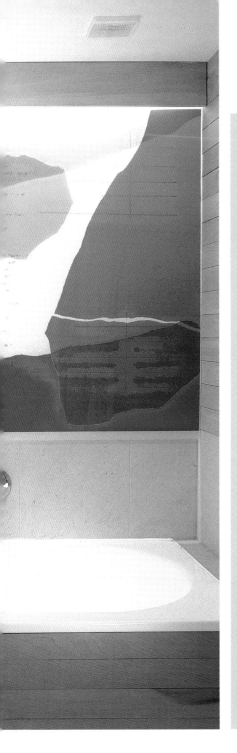

bath screens

If you're showering over the bath, you usually need a means of keeping the water within the bounds of the tub. With a hand-held attachment that you use simply for rinsing soapsuds off yourself and the bath, you could just hold the showerhead low and direct it carefully – and hope for the best! Splashes are inevitable, but they can be limited.

For a ceiling-mounted shower or a shower on a slider rail, you'll definitely need effective protection to stop your bathroom floor flooding. You could go for the cheap and easy option of a shower curtain – but are you prepared to clean it frequently and to replace it regularly? A better option is a solid screen or panel made of tempered or safety glass.

fixed screen

This is an immobile screen sealed at the bottom and side. It is more difficult to access the bath, the taps and the inside of the screen for cleaning, but it is less likely to leak.

swing or pivot

Hinged at the side, and with a rubber seal at the bottom, a swing or pivot screen gives easier access to the bath, but if it's not fitted properly, or as the rubber deteriorates, it may leak.

folding screen

When not in use, the best versions fold flat against the wall for total access to the bath. However, if the wall is out-of-true, they may not stay in place, and as with a swing screen, leakage can occur.

sliding

You can recess a bath into an alcove and create a fully enclosed showering area with a sliding screen (see 43).

it's curtains?

Shower curtains have a reputation foir turning smelly and damp, harbouring unsightly and unhealthy mould and mildew, and wrapping wetly around you while you are showering. However, a new generation of heavy-duty PVC curtains are weighty enough not to flap around and some even have integrated mould-inhibitors.

37 showering with style

5 ideas

There's more to choosing a shower than simply picking the one that you like the look of. You must do your homework first and consider practicality, before you can possibly turn to aesthetics.

taking a systematic approach

First of all, you have to understand what kind of water supply system your household uses. Do you have hot- and cold-water storage tanks? Are they in the attic or in the basement? Is your water pumped or does it rely on gravity? Different types of shower are compatible with different plumbing systems, so answering these questions will help you narrow down (or expand) your choice of products. Seek professional advice if you're at all unsure.

under pressure

There's nothing more disappointing than a trickle of water overhead, when you're hoping for a deluge. Make sure you find out your water pressure before you choose a shower (your plumber should be able to help) and then check the manufacturer's guidelines about water pressure requirements for any particular shower. Your water pressure will be linked to the type of water supply system you have, and can be boosted by a pump. In general, you'll need at least 0.1 bar of pressure for an adequate shower, 0.6 bar for a strong flow, and between 2 and 4 bar for a really high-performance showering experience.

superficial values

Although your choice is in some measure influenced by your water system and water pressure, styling may also be a priority. Very few electric showers (see 38) could be classed as design icons, whereas many mixer showers (see 39) and power showers (see 40) have been given the designer treatment, and are more likely to add panache to your bathroom. Electric showers tend to be limited to white plastic boxes: mixer and power showers come in solid brass plated with chrome, nickel, steel, gold or polished brass. The latter metals obviously offer a traditional look, whereas silver metals predominate on pared-down modern designs.

out of sight

A valve controls the flow of water: this is
the part you open and close by turning
the handle, dial or tap. Choose from an
exposed valve, which protrudes from
the wall, or a concealed model – buried
in the wall and covered with an
attractive plate, which sits flush with the
surface. Concealed valves are neater
looking and the pipework that runs from
the valve to the fixed showerhead is
also hidden – ideal for minimalist and
contemporary bathrooms.

testing the temperature

Valves are either manual (the action of
turning a handle operates the valve) or
thermostatic (a thermostat detects
changes in temperature and opens and
closes the valve automatically to
compensate for fluctuations).
Thermostatic valves are more expensive
but they are an excellent safety measure
and are particularly needed on mixer
showers where the cold water can
suddenly divert to another source (for
example, when a tap is turned on) and
possibly cause scalding.

electric showers 38

Popular in some countries, unheard of in others, the electric shower requires only a cold-water feed to work. If you have good mains pressure (see 8 and 37), it's a simple matter of plumbing the cold water from the rising main to pass over an electrically heated element in a power pack. This heats the water instantaneously, so it emerges hot from the showerhead. Low or unreliable mains water pressure, or a cold supply from a storage tank, can be boosted with a pump so you receive a satisfactory shower spray.

For a more powerful electric shower, choose a model with a high kilowatt rating of 9.5kW or above. Obviously, given the dangers of mixing electricity and water, electric showers should always be fitted by a qualified professional (see 10).

One disadvantage of electric showers is that the power pack is often an unsightly white plastic box on the wall, though some manufacturers do offer systems that conceal the box for a more streamlined look.

mixer showers 39

Drawing water from both the hot and cold supplies, a mixer shower blends the two feeds to the temperature you want, and provides a flow of regulated warm water to your shower.

It's possible to install a mixer shower if you have stored hot and cold water tanks, or if you have cold mains and

power showers

Like a mixer shower, a power shower combines hot and cold water from the separate feeds and blends it to the required temperature. The main difference is that a power shower is fitted with a booster pump to deliver this water at a faster flow rate. In general, you'll need stored hot and cold water in order to supply the shower with the volume of water it requires, but in some cases, a powerful combination boiler may provide a flow rate that is sufficiently high. Check the exact requirements of your installation with your plumber (see 8) and shower supplier.

Booster pumps are not the most attractive pieces of kit, so they are concealed either as part of the shower (an all-in-one unit) or in a power-shower pack, which can be positioned away from the shower (such as in the loft space or in an airing cupboard). The all-in-one units feature a box on the wall, whereas power shower packs are more discreet and keep the lines of your bathroom clean and sleek.

With a power shower, the commonplace saying that a shower is more economical and less wasteful of water than a bath becomes untrue. Standard models deliver 30 litres per minute – that's 300 litres after a 10-minute shower! You can choose brands with less powerful flow or models that offer a water-conserving feature to restrict the flow rate.

Bear in mind too that if your shower also features body jets (see 41), you could be using 50 litres of water per minute! Check the capacity of your hot water storage tank. Will it run cold while you're still rinsing off the soapsuds?

your water is heated by a combination boiler or similar pressurised heating system.

A mixer valve blends the water and the temperature can be controlled manually, or by a thermostatic valve, which ensures the hot water feed is instantly closed if cold water is suddenly drawn off elsewhere.

shower panels

One of the latest trends in bathrooms is the shower panel. It's a wall-mounted console with an integrated array of showerheads and body jets: the complex plumbing for all these outlets is hidden behind the fascia of the console, and all that is required is a simple connection to the hot- and cold-water feeds. It's as easy to disconnect as to connect, so it means a shower panel is a very flexible, mobile fixture.

advantages

• Easy 'plumb-and-play' installation
• Can go with you when you move house
• Superb hydro-massage experience
• Ideal for wet rooms (see 21) but will also fit into larger shower enclosures

disadvantages

• High-pressure water or pump system required
• High water consumption
• Too bulky for small shower enclosures

Styling of shower panels ranges from boxy models in clinical white acrylic to curvaceous shapes and slimline forms in metallic finishes, coloured glass and even organic wood. Corner models are available as well as flat-backed panels for wall mounting.

You can customise your shower panel with a choice of a fixed overhead shower-rose, a handheld hose and multiple body jets. Look too for useful accessories like lighting, storage shelves on the front, hidden racks or niches behind, and even an integrated radio.

As well as wall-mounted shower panels, you can find floor-standing shower columns, which offer a similar hydro-massage experience. Some columns need wall support behind them, but a few are totally freestanding, and are especially suited to open-plan wet rooms (see 21), for example.

showerheads

As the part of your shower system that actually delivers the water, the showerhead is an extremely functional item; but it also has a major role to play in the aesthetics of your bathroom.

Descending directly from the ceiling, installed on a wall-mounted arm, or wall-mounted at an angle, a fixed showerhead keeps your hands free during showering. However, it's not very flexible in terms of spray direction, and you're likely to get your hair wet even if you don't want to.

A handheld shower is excellent for close-up rinsing and increased flexibility. It's even better if it comes with the option of a slider rail kit, so you can position the showerhead at the angle and height you want, and have both hands free.

In polished or matt chrome or nickel finishes, contemporary showerheads tend to be minimalist in style. Choose between pared-down, stick-shaped models (an ideal microphone for singing in the shower!) or overhead shower-roses with a 25cm diameter for an absolute deluge.

Traditional showerheads are usually plated in polished brass, gold or pewter finishes for classical elegance. Popular styles include the old-fashioned watering-can head or deep-lipped curvaceous shower-roses.

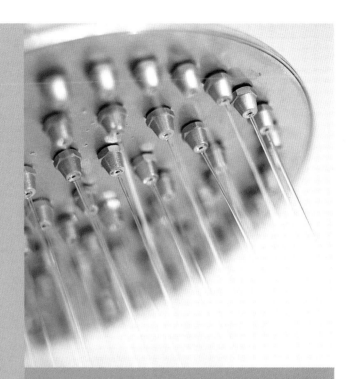

four innovations

Look for these features to increase the functionality of your showerhead.

1 • Adjustable spray patterns: alternate between powerful pulses, soft rain or misting sprays
2 • Massagers: hand-held showerheads with in-built rollers that you rub against your skin
3 • Self-clean heads: pins push through the holes to clear out limescale
4 • Easy-clean heads: soft-plastic nozzles quickly rub clean of limescale

43

shower enclosures

While the basic components remain the same – frame, glass panels, door and tray – the new generation of shower enclosures is a far cry from the white plastic box of early days. Design innovation and superior styling create the ultimate showering experience.

glass act

For safety, glass in shower enclosures should always be toughened, and generally at least 4mm thick. Traditional styles offer patterned or etched glass for privacy, while their contemporary peers promote either crystal clear panels, tints of grey, green or blue, or panes sandblasted or acid-etched for obscurity. As soap sediment and limescale can cause streaking and stains on the glass, look for brands that offer a dirt- and water-repelling coating, to help keep the enclosure looking pristine.

profile piece

The frame or profile of the shower is usually offered in basic white, or a variety of metallic finishes, including polished and matt chrome or gold. The latest look is a natural, wood-effect finish. The most contemporary versions are stripped of a frame altogether, but this means they lack the flexibility of a framed enclosure which has adjustment potential built into the profiles and hinges to make sure that they can create a watertight fit – even when attached to an out-of-true wall.

five entry types

1 • Sliding door: ideal for small bathrooms

2 • Bi-fold door: excellent where space is tight

3 • Pivot door: allows a wide entry but does swing into the room

4 • Corner entry: creates a bigger opening than otherwise possible

5 • Walk-in entry: no door at all (the screen curves to shield the water)

44

shower trays

Designed to catch water and channel it to the waste, shower trays come in a variety of shapes, with sizes starting from about 75cm sq up to 2m-long rectangles. The typical materials are acrylic or fireclay ceramic, but you can also find wood, glass, stone and resin composites, which open up the colour possibilities beyond standard white.

five shower tray shapes

1 • Square (or rectangle): can look boxy, but good for corners or along one wall
2 • Quadrant (or off-set quadrant): this quarter-circle (or elongated quarter-circle) fits neatly into a corner and saves space
3 • Pentangle or neo-angle: a five-sided tray, suits corners in small bathrooms
4 • Circle: usually a freestanding design; looks exciting, but does need space
5 • Contoured: a contoured edge adds interest to a square or rectangular design (often seen in walk-in enclosures)

45

steam cabins

Unlike a shower enclosure, which is open at the top, a steam cabin is a completely sealed unit with tray, glass panels, door and roof. This creates a watertight cocoon where you can indulge in hydrotherapy at home (see 20).

A basic shower cabin will include a fixed overhead shower and/or a handheld shower on a slider rail. Hydro-massage versions add multiple targeted body jets, while spa-style steam cabins offer a Turkish bath experience, which will cleanse your pores, detoxify your body and clear your airways. Further indulgence includes aromatherapy diffusers, coloured lights (chromotherapy), music systems, infra-red heat – and, of course, a comfortable seat to sit on. The best and biggest models are double cabins for shared pleasure.

46 follow your basin instincts

The basin is a fundamental bathroom fixture, a water receptacle for easy cleansing of hands and face. But from its basic origins – a simple bowl to hold water – it has evolved into a sophisticated and design-conscious bathroom centrepiece.

raison d'être

The first question you should ask yourself is what purpose your basin will serve. Is it for hand-washing only? Or also where you'll wash your face, and even your hair, or clean your teeth? How you use the basin will help you decide what size and shape you need.

dare to be different

The days of the matching bathroom suite are gone. Make the basin a focal point, featuring unusual materials such as glass, stainless steel or wood, rather than white ceramic (see 47).

support structure

There are three principal ways to support a basin: on a pedestal, set into or on top of a piece of furniture, or by fixing it to a wall. Each of these alternative approaches has advantages and drawbacks, so consider the practical implications when making your decision (see 48–50).

follow the lines

Basins with strong rectilinear shapes look stunning, but curved bowls may be more practical. Remember sharp internal angles will make cleaning your basin more difficult (see 51).

the scale of the problem

If your bathroom suffers from limescale, unless you're prepared to clean the basin every day to maintain its shiny finish, opt for a slick, easy-clean surface, and a shape that prevents water from pooling at the bottom or on ledges around the sides.

shallow waters

If you live in an area where there is high water pressure, a shallow basin might prove impractical, forcing the water to splash and swirl out. In addition, the positioning of the tap can exacerbate the amount of splashing. Consider a deeper basin with a gentler slope, and perhaps a tap with a flow restrictor to mitigate the problem.

surround about

Not all basin designs incorporate wide ledges where you can rest a bar of soap or anything else you like at hand. Wall-mounted soap dishes or liquid soap dispensers, special toothbrush holders and glass shelving bring essential items within reach and keep basin ledges clear for easy cleaning.

two's company

In an en suite shared by a couple, it's always worth considering installing two basins, side-by-side, if there is space available. Just think: no more banging elbows or waiting impatiently to brush your teeth!

my bowl runneth over

Although most basins have an overflow (which ensures if the tap is left running with the plug in, there won't be a flood), not all do. Check the model you are buying. An overflow is vital if there are children in the house – or absent-minded adults!

waste not

Instead of a plastic plug on a chain, choose a pop-up waste. A lever on the mixer tap operates the metal plug, keeping lines clean and surfaces smooth. An alternative is the spin waste (which sits in the plughole and swivels open or closed when you touch it). Although it looks very minimal and neat, the drawback is you have to plunge your hand into dirty water to operate it.

material world

ceramic

Vitreous china basins offer an extensive choice of sizes, styles and shapes.

advantages
- Non-porous and hygienic
- Easy to clean, particularly with special glazes that repel water and dirt
- Wide range of prices

disadvantages
- Will chip or crack if you drop something heavy onto it

stone

Marble and limestone can appear refined or rustic, depending on how the stone is worked.

advantages
- Often bespoke, so you can specify the shape, size and style

disadvantages
- Porous (basins will need resealing approximately every six months)
- Heavy: will need strong supports

wood

Wooden basins are usually made from hardwood or marine ply and come in a variety of designs.

advantages
- Softens hard-edged designs
- Hardwoods such as teak are naturally antibacterial

disadvantages
- Wood needs to be sealed and maintained to keep it watertight
- The wood can split if it dries out too much

glass

Beautiful clear or frosted basins are created from tempered glass or laminated safety glass.

advantages
- Appears light and airy, so works well in small spaces
- Non-porous and hygienic

disadvantages
- Shows splashmarks, toothpaste, limescale etc

composite

Made from a mix of crushed minerals and resin, composites are moulded into seamless basins in all shapes and sizes.

advantages
- Hundreds of colour choices
- Can be seamlessly integrated into a composite countertop

disadvantages
- May stain if not cleaned

stainless steel

Reminiscent of prison cells and hospitals, stainless steel basins are sure to add an industrial note to a bathroom.

advantages
- Extremely hygienic

disadvantages
- Shows water marks

48
counter-mounted

The counter in question might be a piece of fitted furniture, a freestanding bureau or even a cantilevered shelf.

Typical placement styles are:
- **Lotus-mounted**: the bowl perches on top of the counter
- **Semi-inset**: the bowl is set into the counter, with the front edge protruding
- **Under-mounted**: the bowl is set below the surface of the counter
- **Integrated**: the bowl joins seamlessly with the counter, for example, in the case of a glass or composite option

A surrounding counter gives you the benefit of storage around the basin, and the pipework and waste trap will be hidden if the furniture has doors.

49
on a pedestal

Pedestal basins typically comprise a ceramic bowl sitting on a matching ceramic pedestal, which runs to the floor. This pedestal has a dual function, as it conceals the pipework beneath the basin, but also supports the weight of the heavy ceramic bowl.

In terms of design, the shape of the pedestal will usually echo the style of the ceramic bowl, taking on either traditional or contemporary detailing. Occasionally, you'll find a combination of materials used to stunning effect, such as a glass or ceramic bowl perched on a stainless steel leg.

Although pedestal basins look neat and clean, you will find that dust and dirt gather at the base, which is tricky to clean behind.

50
wall-mounted

The trend for wall-mounting the basin rather than using a supporting pedestal continues to grow. It's not suitable for all bathrooms though, as a heavy basin will require a strong wall to bear the weight.

advantages
- Keeps the floor clear for cleaning
- Makes the room feel more spacious
- Can be set at whatever height you want

disadvantages
- Requires structural work to install support frame
- Wall may need to be strengthened

Bear in mind too that the pipes and waste trap will be visible. You can either conceal these with a ceramic semi-pedestal or stainless steel shroud, or pay extra for chrome-plated feature plumbing.

51

shapes and sizes

If you're plagued by indecision as you survey the vast choice of basin shapes and sizes, make your selection based on practical design parameters – what fits where? what's easy to clean? – as well as personal preferences.

round and curvy

Designs based on the form of a circle are big news at the moment. Whether it's a round glass bowl perched on a vanity unit or a ceramic basin on a full-length pedestal, curves add a soft note to a bathroom. They tend to be easy to clean as there are no internal corners where dirt can collect.

strictly straight

Seemingly inspired by the butler sink from the kitchen, many bathroom basins display rectilinear geometry. In ceramic or stone, these trough-like rectangles and squares share the same heavy proportions and robust styling as their kitchen cousins, and are often found

seeing double 52

It's not unusual for a couple to use an en-suite bathroom together, and in a family bathroom, you'll often see several children crowding in at one time. Elbows tend to get knocked and tempers are liable to get particularly frayed around the basin.

Imagine the luxury of being able to brush your teeth in a leisurely manner, not worrying about hands darting in to turn your cold water hot – or someone aiming poorly when they spit their toothpaste! The ideal solution is to have twin basins.

Obviously, your plans may be halted by space limitations. In a small bathroom, you're struggling to fit in a basin, bath and WC, let alone an additional item. In which case, try at least to keep your single basin relatively free of obstacles around it, so that two people can stand at either side.

In a mid-sized bathroom, compromise comes in the form of a wide basin, where two people can comfortably stand next to each other. You can even find one-piece basins that are divided internally to form two separate sinks.

And if you're fortunate to have a generous amount of space, look at placing twin bowls on a long vanity unit (see 66) or standing matching pedestal basins side-by-side. Yes, you'll double your costs on the basins, the wastes and the taps, but the benefits you gain in terms of convenience – and time saved during an early morning bathroom rush – make it worth it.

perched on wooden counters or wall-mounted for an architectural look. Internal angles can harbour dirt and make cleaning a little more difficult.

best of both worlds

A mixture of straight lines and curved edges define most basin designs, particularly the traditional D-shape of the ceramic pedestal basin.

cornering the market

Quadrant-shaped corner basins are a great solution in a small bathroom. Slotting into the right angle of a room, the corner basin makes use of an otherwise wasted space.

big and little

Basin widths vary from about 30cm for a cloakroom model to a massive 100cm for a focal point trough. About 45–60cm is the norm, though, and provides an ample washbasin for most purposes. Of equal importance is the projection of the basin. A large washbasin may project 60cm into the room, a compact version only 40cm and a tiny hand-rinse basin perhaps only 25cm.

turned on by taps

A small detail like a tap can make or break a design, so be prepared to spend time – and money – on that perfect accessory. You want beautiful form, a design that won't date too quickly, and a degree of functionality that will make your life as easy as possible.

old and new

If your bathroom scheme is classical, it makes sense to choose a period-style fitting, such as Art Deco or Edwardian. But it can also be fun to play with design a little. For example, you could choose a tap that makes reference to old designs (e.g., a bridge mixer – see 54) but offers a contemporary silver-finish (such as matt chrome – see 55). And if you do opt for something ultra-modern for your contemporary bathroom, don't sacrifice functionality. Some designs pare the form down so much that the controllability is sacrificed (can you grip that tiny lever?).

under pressure

Before you buy a tap, find out your water pressure (see 8). Many designs, particularly mixer taps, are suited to high-pressure systems only. Others are specific to low pressure, so be sure you know what you're buying – mistakes can be costly. Also ask your plumber if your hot and cold water are balanced. A mixer tap only functions properly if there's equal pressure in both feeds.

eco-aware

In this more environmentally conscious age, some manufacturers are helping us save water. If you have a high-pressure system, look for a tap with an aerator. This metal mesh restricts the flow of water and oxygenates it to produce a bubbly flow that feels 'bigger' than it actually is.

take cover

If you are buying a high-quality tap – and paying a lot of money for it – you expect it to last. Check that the tap is covered by a product warranty (generally 5–10 years) to give you peace of mind.

tap technology

• Ceramic discs: Increasingly, ceramic disc valves are replacing the traditional screw-down valve and rubber washer. (A valve is the part of the tap that opens and closes to allow water through.) A ceramic disc allows a full flow of water with minimum movement (usually only a quarter-turn from off to fully on) and is much more durable than rubber washers, which tend

to wear away and cause the tap to leak. However, be slightly cautious if you are in a hard-water area. A ceramic disc can be damaged by excessive particles of limescale or other sediments – and unlike a rubber washer, it's not cheap to replace.

• Thermostatic valves: A thermostatic valve reacts to changes in the water temperature, so if the cold flow is suddenly diverted (to the washing machine, for example), it immediately reduces the hot water flow to prevent scalding. It can be set to maintain a temperature you find comfortable. You are more likely to find these on a bath tap than a basin mixer (see 54), as they tend to be linked to bath/shower mixer systems.

• Infra-red sensors: If you can't decide between a lever or a cross-head to turn on your tap, why not go for the ultimate in tap technology? An infra-red, hands-free tap. Moving out of the hospitality sector and into the private bathroom, these turn on and off with a wave of the hand and are extremely hygienic!

54
tap styles

Pillar taps (where the hot and cold taps are separate units) have been overtaken in popularity by the mixer tap. Here, hot and cold water are blended to emerge from a single spout. No more filling a basin to achieve a warm mix of water, or dashing your hands between streams of scalding and freezing water from separate taps.

a medley of mixer taps

• One-hole or monobloc mixer: the spout and controls (which may be handles, heads or levers) form part of a single unit
• Two-hole mixer: the spout is separate from the single control, which operates both temperature and flow rate
• Three-hole mixer: the spout and the hot and cold controls are all separate units

55
tap finishes

You may hear designers or bathroom retailers refer to taps as brassware. Confusingly, they may even be pointing at a chrome-plated tap when they do so. The reason is that taps (and shower fittings) traditionally are made of brass, which is then plated with a hardwearing and attractive metal finish: silver or gold in colour.

Silver-coloured taps are commonly plated in chrome or nickel, though platinum, aluminium, steel and even genuine silver-plating can be found. The latest trend in silver metals sees polished surfaces being superseded by matt or satin finishes. These hide splash marks better and are easier to clean.

Gold-coloured taps are generally perceived as being a traditional choice, and sometimes even a little glitzy. The finish itself might be

• Bridge mixer: the hot and cold pipes join in a bridge shape, with a central spout for the blended water

It's important to test a tap before you buy. How does it feel? Will it grip with a soapy hand? A simple cross-head design is probably the most effective in this regard, but for ease of use – particularly if you suffer from arthritis, for example – try out a lever-style. You don't need nimble fingers or particular strength to push it on and off, though it can be fiddly to adjust the flow rate or temperature precisely.

A simple head that crowns the tap can form a joystick-style control. The streamlined look is excellent on modern and minimal styles and it means there are no fussy bits to clean. However, as with lever taps, a degree of precision is needed to find the right temperature and water flow – and even to return the head to the off-position.

real gold (true indulgence!) or more commonly polished brass, or a brass alloy. These yellow metals are all quite soft, so will scratch and, eventually, may show signs of wear. But gold-hued taps have a visual warmth, which is lacking in silver-coloured taps.

brassed off

• Solid brass is reassuringly heavy. If you pick up a tap that feels light in your hand, put it back down and walk away. Don't let a cheap and flimsy plastic tap spoil your bathroom.
• For a super-hard exterior, look for PVD (physical vapour deposition), a process that bonds a finish to the tap that protects the metal-plating, and is claimed to be eight times harder than chrome and twice as hard as steel.
• Not only can you find mixage finishes where, for example, chrome is accented by gold, but the latest versions mix polished and matt metals of the same colour.

taps in position

The design of your bath or basin may influence where you put your taps. Some come pre-drilled with tap-holes, and although you can cap these off, it can look slightly 'amateur' and can spoil the smooth lines of the basin or bath.

If holes come pre-drilled, do consider filling them with taps, not caps. Old baths might have only two holes provided, but you don't have to settle for old-fashioned pillar taps that supply hot and cold water separately (see 54). You could, for example, choose a bridge mixer (see 54) or have a further hole drilled for a central mixer spout.

If you're buying a brand new bath or basin, you may be given the option of choosing how many tap holes – if any – you want, and where you want them. For the streamlined look that wall-mounting offers, opt for no holes. But if you want to deck-mount your taps, ask yourself whether you want them to perch on the rim of the bath or basin, or to sit alongside on, for example, a tiled counter. And do you want the taps positioned centrally or at the foot end of the bath, or offset at one side of the basin?

wall-mounted

Wall-mounted taps protrude from the wall, with the horizontal spout projecting over the bath or basin.

advantages
• Easier to clean the basin or bath
• No water (or limescale) pooling at base of tap
• Clean-lined look; pipes are buried in wall

disadvantages
• Early planning required (or you'll have to rip tiles off wall)
• If basin or bath does not butt up against the wall, the water from your hand will drip onto the countertop or bath surround

deck-mounted

Deck-mounted taps stand vertically on the rim of the bath or basin, or closely alongside on a counter, for example.

advantages

• No disruption of walls to bury pipes, and therefore less expensive and less time-consuming to install
• Easier to access should there ever be a problem
• Easier to change
• Basin taps can be positioned wherever suits you best – left, right or centre

disadvantages

• More difficult to clean the bath or basin (or countertop)
• Water can collect around the base, causing staining and mould

floor-mounted

Floor-mounted taps are elevated on risers or stand pipes that run to the floor.

advantages

• A great solution for a freestanding bath, or even for a basin positioned away from the wall

disadvantages

• You'll drip water on the floor as you reach for the tap with wet hands
• You'll need to run the plumbing under the floor

Think about the projection of your bath or basin spout. As you lean over a basin to wash your face, you don't want to bang your head on a long spout. Likewise, if you're positioning the bath taps at the centre of the long edge (which makes particular sense if you've opted for a double-ended bath [see 27] for shared bathing – no more arguments about who gets the tap end!), it could impinge on your showering area, for example. But on the other hand, you don't want the water to dribble down the side of the bath or basin. Go for a happy medium.

first impressions

If at all possible, don't make the toilet the first thing you see when you open the bathroom door. Unfortunately, you may be restricted by the size and shape of your bathroom, or by the positioning of the soil pipe. The WC needs to connect to this pipe which carries waste and water away. It can be expensive to move the soil pipe and difficult to extend it.

in a tight corner

If space is limited, look for a compact WC, projecting no more 550mm from the wall. Better yet, conceal the cistern within the wall, so only the pan juts into the room. An unusual solution is a corner model with a triangular cistern, which slots neatly into otherwise dead space.

feeling flushed

Think of the water you use every time you flush. Thankfully, you have the option of environmentally conscious, dual-flush mechanisms. These allow for a water-conserving, half-flush option, which uses as little as 3 litres of water. For a pared-down look and ease of use, choose a discreet push-button system rather than a handle.

deep clean

Cleaning the loo is no one's idea of fun – but at least some models make life a little easier. Some manufacturers offer special pore-free ceramics and water-repellent glazes, which help keep the inner bowl more free of limescale and germs. Also, look for toilet seats that are designed to clip on and off for easy-access cleaning.

ups and downs

It's the age-old argument between men and women. And it's been solved by technology. There are now loos available with hydraulically operated, self-closing seats, which slowly lower themselves after use. The expense might be worth it, if it saves disagreements!

for your convenience

The loo, the toilet, the WC – call it by what name you will, it's the item of sanitaryware that fulfils the most basic of purposes in the bathroom. Hygiene, accessibility, comfort and practicality are all important considerations.

the wc

The current trend is for ultra-clean, clinically white toilets: lines are sleek and pared-down, a look that not only complements the modern bathroom, but also minimises nooks and crannies where germs can breed. Where and how you position the toilet will also have a great bearing on the look of your bathroom.

close-coupled

The cistern and pan are joined in one complete unit, with the cistern visible above and behind the pan. This requires no structural work to install, but looks bulky and it can be tricky to clean around the pedestal.

back-to-wall

A separate cistern is concealed in a wall or within fitted furniture and the pan butts up against this wall or furniture. Structural alterations can be expensive, and you must ensure that the cistern can still be accessed (see 62). The look is streamlined and appears to enlarge small bathrooms.

wall-hung

The WC, without pedestal, is cantilevered from the wall (see 13). You will require a support bracket and, in some cases, the wall will need to be strengthened to bear the weight. Back-to-wall, wall-hung models offer the ultimate, minimalist look, visually create more space, and make it extremely easy to clean the floor underneath. It also means you can choose the height of the pan, which is good if you're extra tall (or short).

to bidet or not to bidet?

Whether you choose to have a bidet in your bathroom will, in part, depend on your upbringing and where you live. The bidet is viewed with derision and suspicion by some, seen as an everyday hygienic necessity by others.

The bidet sits alongside the WC and most often it will be a partner piece with the same design detailing. You can even get loo and bidet models with matching seats for a fully coordinating look.

And like the WC, the bidet can be wall-mounted, which helps the room to open up visually. In addition, this means that the floor is more accessible and easier to keep pristine.

separate lives 60

Ideally, a home should have a separate WC that is easy for guests to access, as well as having a loo within the main bathroom. If, at present, you have only one bathroom in the family home, it might make sense to separate the WC and create a cloakroom. Think about how you use your home, how many people live there, how often people visit – and then imagine the increased flexibility and ease of use if your bathroom and loo are two separate entities:

• Your relaxing bath will no longer be interrupted by anyone knocking urgently at the door.
• The early morning queue outside the bathroom door will be reduced – one child can be brushing his or her teeth at the basin while the other is using the loo next door.
• If you have guests staying, they'll feel less anxious that they may be inconveniencing you while they're in the bathroom.

Creating a separate cloakroom can be as simple as erecting a partition wall within the bathroom, and installing another door accessed from the corridor. As some stud walls can be rather flimsy, it's worth considering creating something more solid, or at least with a degree of soundproofing, to allow greater privacy.

Not all bathroom layouts will allow this simple but effective solution. In which case, could the space necessary for the loo be borrowed from an adjacent room? Or could a nearby cupboard be converted into a cloakroom? Obviously, these structural alterations will be costly, messy and time-consuming, and you must take into account the potential problems associated with moving or extending a soil pipe. Only you can decide if the upheaval will be worth it and if it will result in a more practical, easy-to-live-in home.

privacy please

61

In a family home, or with a couple sharing, privacy in the bathroom can become a precious and much-missed commodity. The door is often left unlocked, or even open, and it's common for the room to be used by more than one person at a time. But sometimes it's nice to have a little privacy.

If it's not possible to create a separate cloakroom to house the WC, screening off the loo within the bathroom goes at least some way to establishing a private zone. This can be done in such a way that the partition becomes a positive design feature.

a glass screen

A sheet of frosted glass, supported by brackets or cemented in place, offers a good level of opacity to discreetly conceal the loo, but it has the benefit of being translucent so light won't be obstructed.

a wall of glass bricks

Like a glass screen, this offers privacy without blocking the light. It is also relatively easy to install and can be built by a proficient amateur.

a partition wall

A half-wall or ceiling-high partition effectively screens the toilet area from the rest of the bathroom. Alcoves can be built into the wall to offer display storage, accessible from either side of the partition. These alcoves also make the wall seem less imposing.

store and order

Cupboards are the staple of bathroom storage, and come in all sizes, shapes, materials and colours. You can choose fitted furniture, freestanding units or wall-mounted cabinets, with a variety of compartments and drawers inside. But there many more options that help you tidy away the bathroom clutter . . ..

freewheeling

A mobile unit gives you maximum flexibility within your bathroom design. Tuck it neatly away beneath the basin or alongside the bath whenever it's not in use, and pull it out into the open when you need to access the contents.

good medicine

The medicine cabinet keeps pills, tablets, bottles of medicine and first-aid equipment together in one safe place, out of children's hands. You can find versions that are clearly medicine-specific (with a red cross on the front, for example) or simply use a small general-purpose wall cabinet with a door – and preferably a lock.

between the walls

If you have a small bathroom, every centimetre of space is important. Consider setting alcoves into the walls, to a depth of about 10cm, to create a shallow storage recess.

blissful bathing

If you set the bath into a furniture surround, you'll create a perimeter shelf, where your soaps and body scrubs can sit within immediate reach. No more having to clamber, dripping wet, out of a hot bath to fetch them from a cupboard.

rack it up

Within reach of the shower or bath, you're bound to need a selection of shampoos and shower gels and a variety of sponges and loofahs. Wall-mount chrome- or brass-plated baskets or install a rack with compartments designed to hold all those necessities at hand.

hideaways

As an alternative to concealing a toilet cistern in a false wall, you can hide it away inside specially designed furniture. Slim units run from the floor to just above cistern height, creating a streamlined look with a push-button flush. A removable panel on the front or top allows access to the cistern for maintenance.

bin it

Tired of picking clothes off the bathroom floor? A laundry bin certainly makes life easier. The traditional wicker basket is now rivalled by smart wooden and metal freestanding containers, some of which double as seats. An alternative is to conceal the laundry bin, often a strong linen bag or a wire mesh container, within a cupboard.

basket cases

Add an organic note to a bathroom with baskets woven from willow or cane. Stack them on the floor with bales of towels inside, place them on shelves to discreetly hold spare toilet rolls or put them in cupboards to compartmentalise the interior.

reading material

Rather than letting magazines and newspapers clutter up the floor, opt for a wall-mounted magazine holder, or a stylish multi-purpose rack that also includes a toilet roll holder and a loo brush.

safe and secure

As well as storing cleansing lotions and potions for your body, you'll often want to keep bathroom cleaning agents, detergents and bleach close at hand. For these, you'll need concealed storage (they're not the most attractive bottles) and preferably a lockable cabinet if you have young children in the house.

10 ideas

63 furniture features

Bathroom furniture used to be unimaginative and unvaried: an imposing bank of white lacquer units, with fussy detailing and yet a blandly uniform appearance. The reality now, amid ranges of fitted, freestanding and modular furniture, is an exciting choice of colours and materials, with slick exterior finishes and intelligent internal storage solutions.

Materials vary, but finishes include water-resistant, foil-wrapped doors in wood effects, an extensive colour choice of lacquers, or even acid-etched glass or matt aluminium panelling. Work surfaces are also high-performance to ensure that water spillages don't penetrate and that knocks and scratches can be tolerated. Solid surface composites, high-pressure laminates with waterproof backing and toughened glass are some of the principal options.

Most ranges present the opportunity of external accessories like splashbacks, lighting and mirrors. Obviously, these extras add to the price, but they do help provide complete solutions for your bathroom needs.

The variety of internal storage solutions for bathroom furniture now rivals that of the kitchen. When you open the doors you'll find corner carousels, pull-out racks, integrated laundry bins, waste bins and compartmentalised drawers all designed to conceal your bathroom clutter behind a calm exterior.

access all areas

Check that the bathroom furniture you buy incorporates access panels so that your plumbing can be checked and maintained with the minimum of fuss. You should be able to quickly unscrew or clip-off the panel to reach the pipes beneath the bath or basin, or the cistern of your back-to-wall loo.

64

fitted furniture

The days of solid banks of cupboards overpowering a bathroom design are gone. Now, fitted furniture is trying not to look so . . . fitted. Yes, you can still opt for a run of base units stretching from wall-to-wall, but it's much more visually stimulating to mix-and-match using a selection of versatile pieces.

base units

These floor-standing cabinets are the staple elements of any range of fitted furniture. For a less heavy look, opt for plinth-free designs with stylish chrome legs, or a recessed plinth that gives the impression of 'floating'. You can even wall-mount units to free up the floor, making the room feel more spacious (see 13) and cleaning easier. Select a variety of depths, such as a slimline 20cm where space is tight or a comfortable 50cm to inset a basin. You can also vary the 'skyline' with a range of heights.

wall units

Head-height storage is easy to access (and can keep things out of children's hands). To make wall units seem less uniform and imposing, select a variety of heights, widths and depths. Use frosted-glass doors for a lighter look and consider how they will open – sliding doors or upwards-bi-folding doors will be more space-saving.

small concerns

If you have a small bathroom, your first thought may be that squeezing in furniture will make the space even more cramped. However, slimline fitted furniture can have the opposite effect. Use a bank of units with a depth of about 20cm to conceal the toilet cistern, to hide away pipes and to form a support for a semi-inset basin. Streamlining one wall of the room can make the space appear deceptively large.

freestanding furniture 65

The popularity of freestanding bathroom furniture lies in its flexibility. Different elements can be moved around the room should your needs change – or if you simply want to try a different layout. You can bring in new items as and when you can afford them, or if you decide later that you need more storage. And when you move house, you can take your furniture with you.

Another reason to choose freestanding pieces is that a few select elements can look less imposing than a traditional, wall-to-wall bank of fitted cabinets (though with the varied looks of the latest collections of fitted bathroom furniture, the distinction between freestanding and fitted has become extremely blurred).

Prime pieces of freestanding furniture for your bathroom might include:
• low sets of pull-out drawers – ideal for towels, and useful to sit on too
• trolley units that can be wheeled out from under basins or pushed next to the bath whenever you need a 'bathside' table
• tall cupboards with lots of shelving inside for bottles and boxes
• basin stations – a bureau or table that supports a basin and provides storage beneath (see 66)
• laundry bins, so dirty clothes and wet towels aren't left lying on the floor
• storage chests – ideal for towels and they make great seats, too

It's common for ranges of bathroom furniture to offer both freestanding and fitted items, allowing you to create a modular look in your bathroom. Imagine a bank of wall-fixed fitted base units with a complementary laundry bin or matching wheeled trolley that can be moved where you wish.

66 vanity units

As its name suggests, the vanity unit is the area of the bathroom dedicated to primping and preening. For women, it has replaced the bedroom dressing table. And for men? Well, give them a mirror and they can beautify with the best of them!

The basic elements of a vanity unit are a mirror, good lighting, a basin and handy storage. By bringing together these four elements, you can create your own personal beauty and grooming zone.

basin stations

A basin station is a dual-function piece of furniture that combines a bathroom basin with storage solutions. In its basic form it's a table with a basin set on or in it. The tabletop around the basin provides an easily accessed area for soap, toothbrushes, make-up etc, and shelving beneath keeps larger items at hand. A towel rail at the front or side is a useful additional feature.

67 on the wall, in the wall

It's common to see cabinets and shelves attached to a wall, but you can also make use of the space within the wall itself to create shelving recesses or feature alcoves.

why use walls?
- Clears the floor area for a sense of space
- Storage can be fixed at eye-level height
- Items can be placed out of reach of children

Shelves are one of the simplest forms of storage. Choose narrow glass shelves on chrome brackets, hefty wooden slabs on wrought-iron supports, or even gloss-painted, double-thickness MDF, cantilevered from the wall. It's best to combine shelving with cabinets so you can hide away general bathroom paraphernalia, otherwise be prepared to keep everything neat. Rolled-up towels and attractive bottles can look stylish.

mirrored cabinets

A mirrored wall-unit above the basin is invaluable for applying make-up, shaving or putting in contact lenses. Look for one with integrated lighting and sockets (for an electric razor or an electric toothbrush), but remember that it will need to be wired in.

waterproofing your walls 68

It makes sense to choose a specialist finish for your bathroom walls that will withstand steam and humidity, occasional splashes and drips – or even regular torrents of water. Before you make your decision, consider the points below.

how wet will it get?

The first question to ask yourself is how much water will come into contact with your walls. Areas near the basin and bath are bound to suffer occasional splashes, for example, even if adults are using them. If children are involved, the splashes will be more frequent – and bigger! And the walls of a shower enclosure must be fully waterproofed, of course. Also, take account of the effects of steam. If you (and other members of your family) have long, hot showers every day, the bathroom will be frequently exposed to humidity and dampness. Clouds of steam will condense into tiny water droplets on cold surfaces such as walls.

mix and match

Experiment with mixing different wall-coverings according to where the water will splash. One popular approach is the half-tiled wall, where an area up to about head height is tiled, and the rest of the wall painted. Alternatively, you could create a neat splashback behind the basin or on the wall next to the bath – use tiles, wood, glass, stone or laminate – and apply a contrasting wallcovering elsewhere. It's a cost-effective way of waterproofing vulnerable zones, and you can opt for more expensive materials for your splashback as you aren't covering such a large area.

papering over

Generally, wallpaper is not recommended for bathrooms (with the exception of a few specialist moisture-resistant papers). If you have excellent ventilation and low humidity – and if you promise not to splash! – then yes, you can paper the walls. Otherwise, don't be surprised if the paper peels, stains or mildews within a matter of months.

going solo

Most people are capable of picking up a paintbrush, some can even master tiling, but stone cladding or plaster finishes really are best left to the experts. And professional labour costs money (see 4 and 5). If you're not prepared to learn how to tile a bathroom, or don't have time, you could be looking at two or three days labour on top of the initial purchase cost of the tiles. Plaster finishes may be quicker to apply, but finishing them (waxing and polishing) also adds on hours of labour. Always factor in the costs of installation when making your decision.

last, but not least

It can be tempting to forge ahead with preparing and decorating the walls to give your room a finished look. But remember, you may have to gouge out sections of wall to bury pipes or wiring. In your schedule of completion, wall finishes are a cosmetic consideration and should be one of the last items you tackle (see 25 and 26).

69 ceramic tiles

Ceramic tiles are made from a mixture of clays and other minerals, which are shaped and fired to create a stable material. Over centuries, the ancient craft of tile making has evolved to encompass new manufacturing processes and technological developments, and the diversity of ceramic tiles is now unparalleled: designs embrace a myriad of colours, sizes, patterns and shapes.

Ceramic tiles fall into two broad categories: glazed and unglazed. Wall tiles are generally glazed, which means they are coated with a non-porous, protective vitreous coating.

five benefits of glazed tiles

1 • Unlimited colour variations
2 • Stain-resistance
3 • Superior waterproofing
4 • Extremely hygienic
5 • Easy to clean

wall or floor?

Manufacturers usually specify whether tiles are suitable for walls or for floors. Floor tiles are often too thick and heavy to apply to walls, and wall tiles are too delicate to withstand foot traffic – so make sure you're buying tiles suited to the purpose.

Once grouted in place, you won't be able to remove tiles without breaking them. So be cautious if you're following a specific colour trend that may date quickly. Aqueous blues and greens seem to be standing the test of time and white is a classic choice.

Don't just think about colour, but consider size, shape and texture too. All have a bearing on the look of a room. Larger squares can open a room up more, while rectangles running vertically will make a room appear taller. Texture is also very important. It can add visual interest to a plain colour such as white, and tactile interest when you touch the tiles. However, it's best to opt for a subtle texture that won't harbour dirt or germs.

mosaic tiles

70

Roman villas and Byzantine palaces were decorated with mosaic pictures composed of thousands of tiny tiles. Interest in mosaics has been renewed recently, though the elaborate designs of past eras are rarely re-created. It's more usual to cover the walls in mosaic tiles (or tesserae, as they're known) of a single colour or varying shades of one colour, such as a palette of blues. To make application easier, mosaic tiles usually come in web-backed sheets, comprising perhaps 100 tiles or more, so they don't have to be applied individually.

mosaic magic

• Look out for mosaic tiles in stone, metal and glass, as well as ceramic.

• If you find the look of a whole bathroom or wall covered in mosaic tiles overpowering, why not use just a narrow strip of mosaics to define an area?

• Try popping a tile out, at random, from each sheet of mosaic, and replacing it with a single tile of a contrasting colour

glass and 71 metal tiles

Glass and metal tiles have found their place in bathrooms as a complement to the materials that are being incorporated into bathroom design. Acid-etched glass screens, frosted basins, sand-blasted shelves and other accessories can be accented by the use of glass tiles in matching subtle hues. Or you can pick out the gleam of polished chrome shower fittings or the duller sheen of satin-finished taps using tiles with bright silver surfaces.

Some glass tiles are pigmented throughout, while others simply have a coloured backing. You'll find different degrees of tone and translucency, and bear in mind that when applied to a wall, the tiles will lose some of their lustre and may appear to be darker than you first imagined.

Metal tiles are usually ceramic tiles with a metallic glaze, though you may come across some solid metal plates that function as tiles. Silver hues include platinum, stainless steel, nickel, pewter and chrome, but for more warmth choose gold, copper or brass.

It's worth noting that some metals, such as copper and brass, will tarnish unless they are protected by a lacquer coating, and that all metals will scratch if rubbed with an abrasive cleaner and will be damaged by acids, such as some cleansing agents.

wood panelling

The term 'wood panelling' may bring to mind dark and dusty old libraries, but in the bathroom environment, it is typically blond-wood tongue-and-groove that is used (so-called because of the way the boards slot together – a protruding tongue on one fits into a pre-cut groove on the next). Tongue-and-groove has an organic and simple feel and is associated with a robust, outdoorsy aesthetic. Leaving knotty pinewood, for example, in its naked state (apart from a clear varnish sealant) creates a very raw and natural-looking bathroom.

As wood has to be protected from moisture, paint can be used instead of varnish to seal it. Choose a gloss or satin version that is specific to wood – and will resist damp conditions. Colour choices are extensive, though white is always popular, and aqueous blues and greens often feature, especially in marine-themed bathrooms.

Tongue-and-groove is commonly applied to mid- or even three-quarter-height on the walls, but can be over-powering if used too extensively. Although it's a cost-effective way of covering expanses of wall, be restrained and reserve it for small sections, such as behind the bath, and even for the box surround.

new wood

Modernists have abandoned gently old-fashioned tongue-and-groove in favour of veneers of rich cherrywood, grained oak and patterned walnut that are securely fixed to walls and sealed with water-proof lacquer. Equally striking are panels of tropical hardwoods, like iroko and teak. But these water-resistant woods don't come cheap and need occasional re-sealing if they are used close to water. If at all possible, be environmentally responsible and make sure your wood (especially the more exotic species) has been sourced from sustainable forests.

stone surfaces

Stone is so versatile that it is difficult to define it categorically. It can be rustic or refined, traditional or modern, easy-wear or high-maintenance. The only qualities that can be commonly ascribed to all types of stone are durability and unchangeability.

Unlike ceramic tiles, the stone variety are not designed by man. The characteristics of each type of stone are 'designed' by nature, formed millennia upon millennia ago. All we can affect is the shape and size of tile that is cut from the huge sheets and boulders of rock quarried from the earth. After processing, the resultant cladding material ranges from weighty slabs to tiny mosaic tesserae (see 70).

Bathroom walls tend to feature four main families of stone: granite, marble, limestone and slate. Each has a particular aesthetic, so the choice will be based as much on personal likes and dislikes, as on any practical reasoning.

granite

- Extremely hardwearing and practical
- Impervious to water
- Mottled or flecked in appearance
- Wide spectrum of colours, particularly darker shades, including black, red, brown and green

marble

- Associated with classical and opulent ambience
- Porous, needs to be sealed
- Usually veined in appearance
- Pure marble is white, but other shades (greys, browns, reds, even black) are also found

limestone

- Offers a calm, soothing, contemporary look
- High porosity, needs to be sealed
- Generally uniform appearance, some slight mottling or fossilisation
- Commonly found in golden, buff and sandy tones, but also white, grey, blue or even chocolate brown

slate

- Works particularly well with rustic or ethnic style
- Waterproof
- Usually a textured surface, crystalline glints, some striping or mottling
- Generally charcoal grey with blue, purple and green variations

Make sure you explain to your supplier that the stone you choose

is for use on walls. Stone is extremely heavy, so your wall-covering needs to be as thin and light as possible. Regular-sized, wall-specific tiles are easier to use than large slabs, but even so, are best applied by professionals who can ensure that sufficiently strong cement is used. If you do want the sophisticated look that outsized slabs offer, you may need your wall strengthened and the slabs will have to be fixed to a special support system.

The whole look of your bathroom will be defined not only by the type of stone you choose – and the size and shape of the tile – but also by the finish given to the stone. A highly polished finish suggests opulence and glamour, and works well with granite and marble; a honed finish (matt-satin) is more subtle and modern, but offers a similarly wipe-clean surface; textured finishes caused by tumbling, bush-hammering or natural pitting offer a raw appearance and will hide splashmarks well, but will be more difficult to keep clean.

74

paint it on

Ordinary vinyl emulsion is not recommended for bathroom walls if there is a chance it will get splashed, as it will show stains and watermarks. Nor will it be resistant to steam and moist conditions, eventually peeling away or being plagued by mould. For this reason, if you are using paint in a bathroom, make sure it's a specialist paint suited for the purpose.

Bathroom-specific paint is usually an acrylic-based eggshell paint or has a latex or plastic content, resulting in a satin or silky sheen that will be resistant to splashes and easy to wipe dry. It's not claimed to be totally waterproof though, so don't be tempted to use it as an alternative to tiles in wet areas.

You can also find paint that has ingredients specifically designed to combat problems associated with bathrooms, such as condensation, mildew and mould. Anti-condensation paint has a semi-permeable surface, allowing the wall to 'breathe', and paint with mould- and mildew-inhibitors is essential if you have a very steamy bathroom or poor ventilation.

advantages

- Relatively inexpensive way of covering a large area
- Quick and easy to apply
- More durable than ordinary emulsion
- Easy to re-paint if you want to change the colour
- Light-reflecting finish expands the bathroom
- May inhibit mould or mildew

disadvantages

- Only water-resistant, not totally waterproof
- The sheen in the paint will highlight less-than-perfect walls
- Limited to a few specific ranges (therefore your colour choice may be limited)
- Often more expensive than non-specific emulsion

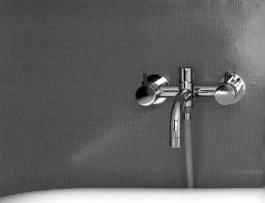

75 polished plaster

Known also as stucco lustro, marmorino or Venetian plaster, polished plaster is a centuries-old wall render that famously adorned Italian palaces and churches. Its smooth, glassy look can be sumptuous and decorative, or with texture and pigmentation, it can appear rustic and weathered.

Polished plaster is particularly suited to bathrooms because it is hardwearing and waterproof. The base, made of lime, cement and marble dust, is given added protection by layers of wax rubbed into the surface.

Application should be left to an expert and you can specify different finishes. Polishing the surface brings the marble dust within the plaster to a smooth, high-gloss; but you can also ask for a pitted or dragged finish, for example, to add textural depth to your walls.

Historically, polished plaster took its hue from the natural, earthy colours of the Mediterranean region, but pigments can be added to tint the material to subtle or saturated colours. The coloured finish is not uniform, but shows variations that add dimension to the room.

advantages

- Waterproof
- Durable
- Can be custom-coloured
- Lots of different finishes

disadvantages

- Can be expensive
- Needs professional application

feet first

Flooring choices for bathrooms are wide-ranging. You can opt for refined ceramic or earthy stone, traditional linoleum or high-tech vinyl, rustic cork or industrial rubber. Their looks and properties vary, but whatever material you choose, think about the practicalities as much as the aesthetics.

naked truth

As you'll be walking on the bathroom floor with bare feet, how it feels to your skin is an important consideration – not only the texture, but the temperature too. If you don't think you can cope with cold stone on a winter morning, perhaps underfloor heating is the answer.

slippery when wet

Take account of the fact that no matter how careful you are, some parts of your bathroom floor will get wet. Obviously, choose materials that are water-resistant, but make sure too that the surface is non-slip or incorporates a texture to give extra grip.

ups and downs

If the floor in your bathroom is a different material to the adjacent room, it may cause problems. For example, if you've laid underfloor heating and thick stone slabs, the bathroom floor might be several centimetres higher than the adjoining carpet. While a difference of a few millimetres can be hidden with a standard threshold strip, unless you want to create a small step up into the bathroom (and risk stubbing your toe until you've learnt the hard way), you'll need to smooth out any greater transitions. Ask your contractor (see 7) for solutions such as a sloped or custom-made threshold strip – or in extreme cases, you may need to raise the adjoining floor to minimise the difference. It's worth thinking about height differences when you're choosing your flooring.

keep it clean

The bathroom is where you go to get clean – not dirty. So you need a floor that is hygienic, and easy to keep free of dirt and germs. For this reason, carpets are really not recommended for bathrooms. Yes, they feel nice underfoot, but they harbour bacteria, dead skin, moulted hair – and if they get wet too often, they will eventually go mouldy and begin to smell.

what lies beneath

The success of your floor covering will depend on the preparation of the subfloor. If you're laying ceramic or stone, you must have a stable subfloor that will not flex or move (otherwise cracks will appear in your tiles on top), such as a concrete screed with a self-levelling compound. Vinyl and linoleum can be laid on to high-quality plywood, but it must be well fitted, smooth and free of dirt, with no gaps between boards, or your flooring above will take on its defects. Your contractor or retailer should be able to advise on the most appropriate type of subflooring.

77 ceramic tiles

Although all ceramic tiles are extremely water-resistant, it is only when tiles are glazed that they become fully waterproof. Some types of floor tiles are unglazed, and will have a degree of permeability.

Unglazed tiles include terracotta and quarry tiles. Quarry tiles are made from a paste of natural clay or shale extruded into shape. Colours are limited to an earthy palette of red, brown and grey. Terracotta has a rich burnt orange or red colour, and the tiles are often hand-made, giving them a raw and honest quality. Traditionally, terracotta tiles are waxed with beeswax to protect them, but there are modern sealants now available.

advantages of unglazed floor tiles

• Less slippy
• Extremely resistant to wear and abrasion
• The colour is the same throughout (so chips won't show)

disadvantages of unglazed floor tiles

• Colour and design options are limited
• Slightly porous unless sealed

The texture of your tiles, whether glazed or unglazed, is important. If the glaze is high gloss and the surface is smooth, the tile will be dangerously slippery when wet. An unglazed tile with a rough finish will have more traction.

five tile tips

1 • Ceramic tiles are hard and unforgiving underfoot. Anything you drop is likely to break, and may damage your tiles.
2 • Don't apply ceramic wall tiles to floors: they will be too thin to withstand people walking on them and will crack.
3 • If you're choosing a glazed ceramic tile, opt for a matt glaze and a slight texture to minimise risk of slipping.
4 • Mosaic tiles are good for floors as the hundreds of grout lines give good traction underfoot.
5 • Grout on floors gets dirty. Consider using a waterproof epoxy grout rather than a more porous (though cheaper) cement-based grout.

stone

Whether your walls are surfaced with mini-mosaics or hefty slabs, the inherent solidity, longevity and natural beauty of stone will be apparent.

granite

With its high quartz content, granite is the hardest stone cladding. This makes it a highly practical floor covering, though its density means it is extremely heavy.

marble

Marble's classical connotations are perfect for a traditional room. It is a soft and porous stone, which will stain and scratch unless properly cared for. It also tends to be slick when wet, so avoid highly polished slabs underfoot.

limestone

Limestone is a beautiful stone, with warm tones and uniform shading – but black-soled shoes, high-heels and water splashes will all take their toll. Most limestones are relatively soft and porous, and will be unforgiving of daily abuse.

slate

Riven slate, which is cleft rather than cut from the rock, has a wonderful irregular texture, which makes it extremely slip-resistant. In addition, slate has superb lateral strength, and a high degree of natural waterproofing.

other choices

Composites, which mix chips or granules of real stone with a bonding agent to produce a hardwearing material, are easier to look after than natural stone. Terrazzo, for example, captures chips of granite or marble in polished mortar. You can even find realistic limestone look-alikes that compound limestone dust with resins.

four considerations

1 • The weight: the joists in your timber floor may need to be strengthened.
2 • The fragility: make sure you prepare the subfloor correctly. Unless it's perfectly smooth and stable, you risk cracking the stones as you step on them.
3 • The temperature: stone is affected by the temperature around it: if the subfloor is cold and damp, the stone will be cold and damp as well.
4 • The maintenance: for stone to keep its good looks, it needs to be cleaned regularly and re-sealed to maintain waterproofing.

vinyl and linoleum 79

Linoleum and vinyl, both manufactured waterproof floor coverings, are often mistaken for each other. They have many similarities in looks, applications, and inherent properties, but differ significantly in construction.

Vinyl truly is a synthetic material. Made from PVC (with some filler compounds in cheaper brands), vinyl is resilient, waterproof, hardwearing, hygienic and easy to clean; all properties that make it an excellent covering for bathroom floors.

You can choose between sheet or tile vinyl. The sheet form is unwieldy and best fitted by an expert, but has the advantage of being seam-free. Tiles are more manageable, and can even be fitted by a proficient amateur. However, care must be taken to ensure the tiles butt tightly up against each other and that adhesive seals the gaps. As water can seep between the tiles if they are not fitted correctly, some manufacturers will only guarantee the product if installed by an approved fitter, which can add to the expense. You can get self-adhesive vinyl tiles, which are cheaper, but these are more likely to move and are less waterproof.

Both cushioned and un-cushioned vinyl are available. The latter is softer underfoot, but will show any marks and dents from high heels or furniture legs, or if anything sharp is dropped on it.

While linoleum is also man-made, the substances used are natural, not synthetic. The material takes its name from linseed oil, one of its prime ingredients, with others being cork, wood flour, resins, chalk, limestone and natural pigments. Sheet linoleum is on pliable jute backing, and the tile variety is on rigid polyester.

Lino shares vinyl's easy-clean properties, and is also hardwearing. In fact, over time, exposure to air hardens it and increases its durability, though it remains relatively quiet underfoot. But unlike vinyl, linoleum is environmentally friendly, being made of recyclable and sustainable raw materials.

And its linseed oil content has a further benefit: the continuous oxidisation of the oil produces a bactericidal effect, making it extremely hygienic in the bathroom. What's more, lino is anti-static, repelling dust and making it easier to clean.

ten reasons to buy vinyl and linoleum

1 • Waterproof
2 • Durable
3 • Easy-clean smooth surface
4 • Quiet and warm underfoot
5 • Can be laid in seam-free sheets
6 • Hygienic
7 • Vast variety of colours and designs (including authentic imitations of stone)
8 • Anti-static (lino only)
9 • Anti-bacterial (lino only)
10 • Eco-friendly (lino only)

but take care with

• Cushioned materials (will show dents)
• Cheaper materials (will show wear/be less waterproof)
• Tiles (will allow water to seep between if not filled properly)
• Sheet (needs expert fitting, and there may be more wastage – plus, if you have a large bathroom, you might have to have a join)

copycat

With vinyl and linoleum you have the possibility of replica ceramic tiles, wood, stone or even metal flooring that offer the aesthetic benefits of those materials, without the issues of maintenance or waterproofing. Modern technology means that these imitations are now extremely realistic. Alternatively, you can take advantage of other technological advances and opt for contemporary digital designs with holographic qualities, highly saturated colours and subtle textures.

wood – and grass! 80

Bathrooms often have a cold, clinical appearance, which can be tempered by the introduction of warm and organic materials, such as wood. The look can be as rustic or as refined as you wish, from wide board oak to open-grained tropical woods or narrow planks of elegant maple or beech.

• Solid hardwood: planks or strips of real wood. It's expensive, but beautiful; may warp in humidity, but can be protected with coats of lacquer; will mark over time, but can be sanded and re-lacquered
• Engineered flooring: a veneer of real wood bonded to layers of particleboard. It's reasonably priced and looks good; more stable than solid wood, especially if lacquered, but may still warp in moist conditions; will mark, but can be sanded and re-lacquered only a limited number of times
• Laminate flooring: a photographic reproduction of wood bonded to layers of particleboard. It's the most affordable option; certain brands are suited to bathrooms and even come with a guarantee; less susceptible to marking or denting than real wood

house of bamboo

Often mistaken for a wood, though in fact it's a grass, bamboo has become big news for bathrooms. Layers of bamboo strips are laminated under high pressure to produce a flooring material that looks very like a wood, but has properties that make it much more suitable for bathrooms. Namely, it is much more stable than wood flooring, and won't shrink or swell noticeably in a moist atmosphere.

With its distinctive linear markings, bamboo is unusual and attractive. Its typical colour is honey-blond, but it can be pressure steamed for a darker shade. In addition, it is a very environmentally friendly product, as bamboo grass is plentiful and extremely fast growing.

cork

81

Cork flooring is undergoing something of a design revival, perhaps due to its value-for-money price and its eco-friendliness. Its new look combines warm charm with contemporary aesthetics.

Comprising about 50% air, cork offers excellent shock absorbency and soundproofing, but is permeable to water unless sealed. Some companies supply cork tiles with a coating of durable, waterproof (though not eco-friendly) PVC. Otherwise, your floor will require four or five layers of sealant. Once sealed, cork is easy to clean, needing only a quick sweep and a damp mop.

You can find pigmented cork that takes the colour palette beyond the neutral browns, or even cork-backed tiles finished with patterned or photographic digital images protected by PVC.

rubber

82

Hardwearing and waterproof, industrial-style rubber flooring has now moved into bathrooms. You can find synthetic, natural and recycled rubber flooring, all with similar properties: warmth, softness and hygiene. Tiles are easier to lay than rubber on a roll, but will have more joins where water could penetrate. An alternative is a poured rubber floor, but this will need professional installation.

As rubber becomes slick if wet, look for a textured anti-skid surface, such as a pattern of studs, dimples or tread-plate effect. You'll be spoilt for choice with colours, from industrial grey to marbled mixes of bright hues.

Keep your rubber flooring shining with applications of specialist polish, clean it with a damp mop and buff it dry afterwards.

let there be light

A successful lighting scheme should harmonise so well with the way you use the room that you probably won't even notice how effective it is. You're more likely to comment on poor illumination than good lighting.

laying down the ground rules

Before you can begin to plan your lighting scheme, you must finalise your bathroom design (see 11). After all, it's no good installing mirror lighting and then realising you want the mirror on the opposite wall. The position of the bath, basin and shower will guide your scheme, as will any special features such as recesses or alcoves.

variations on a theme

A single pendant light in the centre of the ceiling provides the most basic illumination. It might even seem sufficient for a small bathroom. But how much more visually exciting – and how much more useful – to have a variety of lighting, such as uplights, downlights and wall-washers. Layers of lighting, some diffused and some directed, make every area of the bathroom accessible.

feeling flexible

Having decided you'll have more than one light source in the bathroom, make the decision to have separate controls for different lighting. That way, you can decide to switch off the bright halogen downlights if you want to lie back in the bath and relax – no getting dazzled when you look at the ceiling. Instead, turn on some mood-enhancing uplights or an accent light.

If you have a dimmer switch installed, you'll be able to control the ambience even more. And a dimmer will be especially useful when you're entering the bathroom from a dark bedroom in the middle of the night or early in the morning, allowing your eyes to adjust slowly.

sources of light

• Natural light is the best source of illumination, though in bathrooms it will often be diffused by a window treatment or blocked altogether, which means you'll have to resort to artificial illumination even during the daytime.

• Tungsten filament is the most common form of domestic lighting. When electricity passes through the tungsten filament in the bulb, the filament glows, producing a hot, incandescent light. The light is yellowish in appearance, which means it's warm-toned.

• Tungsten halogen is a variation on tungsten filament. Halogen gas is trapped within the bulb, and reacts with the heated filament to produce a much whiter and brighter light.

• Fluorescent light has a bad reputation in bathrooms. It's generally unflattering and flickering – not what you want as you peer in the mirror. However, a new generation of compact fluorescents are flicker-free and some even mimic natural daylight.

safe and sound

It's obvious, but it bears repeating, water and electricity are a dangerous mix. For this reason, rules and regulations (which differ from country to country) are in place to protect you. Involve a qualified electrician in your lighting design and he'll be able to advise you on your scheme and even carry out the installation (see 10). A few general points to bear in mind are:

• Water-resistant lights: any fitting that might get wet will need to be sealed. You can get fully waterproof lights for shower areas, for example, and water-resistant lights for other areas of the bathroom. If you choose a pendant light, you might not think it needs to be water-resistant. However, even one splash of cold water can cause a hot bulb to shatter, so it's worth protecting the bulb.

• Switches: in some countries (the UK, for example), you can't have switches in the bathroom (only pull-cords). Check your local regulations about different types of switches and where you're allowed to position them (see 10).

84 ambient lighting

Obviously, the prime function of lighting in the bathroom is to allow us to see; but that basic fact aside, illumination can also be used to set a mood and even as a decorative effect. Light can create shadows, highlight textures, cast patterns and add a new dimension to a surface. So take both practical and aesthetic functions into account when you plan your lighting scheme.

three questions to ask yourself

1 • How much natural light enters the bathroom? Is it via a window or a skylight? Does it enter all year round? Do you currently block it with a window dressing?

2 • Do you use the bathroom in the dark hours of the morning? During the day? Late at night?

3 • Do you want your bathroom to wake you up and refresh you? Do you like to relax and unwind in the bathroom? Does your mood vary?

Obviously, if the bathroom has no window at all or if you have to totally block it to stop neighbours seeing in, you'll need to create some 'daylight' by artificial means. A skylight is perhaps the best means of letting natural light into the room, but at night, you'll still need to switch on a light.

Most people will use the bathroom at different times of day; early morning before they leave for work, late at night before going to bed. In the morning, you usually want to be refreshed – but not blinded – by light. In the evening, you want to be able to soak in a tub with atmospheric lighting to soothe you.

There's no hard and fast rule about how many lights you need for a particular size of bathroom, nor how bright or how dim they need to be. But in general, err on the generous side and build in flexibility so that you can alter the level of illumination – and the areas that are illuminated – according to your need.

Uplights are an excellent means of creating a sense of space. Reflecting off a white-painted ceiling, they seem to heighten the bathroom. They can be wall-mounted or set into a surface such as a shelf or even the floor. On the floor, they'll need to be in fully sealed casings in case of water spillages. Also, choose a low-voltage light that won't get too hot, as you'll probably walk over it with bare feet. And finally, make sure the light is positioned so it doesn't shine directly into your eyes (for example, as you bend over the basin).

Balance uplights with downlights, such as pendant spotlights and recessed halogen spots. Position one over the bath or basin for the effect of light on rippling water. A series of recessed ceiling lights close to the edge of the ceiling act as wall-washers, creating a scalloped pattern of light arches on the wall.

task lighting

Task lighting is the most purposeful type of illumination and in bathrooms it usually centres on the mirror to help with general grooming, as well as more specific activities such as shaving, applying make-up and putting in contact lenses.

mirror lighting

You want to be able to peer closely at your reflection without your face being shadowed. Light from a single direction, such as a downlight over the basin, will cast shadows in your eye-sockets and below your nose.

If a downlight is all you have, at least angle it towards the mirror. Light will be reflected back on your face and will minimise shadows. A better solution is to provide even, diffused light from either side, such as two halogen strip lights (or tungsten for a warmer glow). These can also be balanced by a downlight above.

Look for mirrors with integrated lighting – some even have a full perimeter of recessed light, which ensures that the face is illuminated from every angle.

three other places for task lighting

1 • The bath: if you like to lie in the bath and read, you'll need a good source of light above your head.
2 • The shower: recessed shower enclosures can be terribly dark and dingy. A fully sealed overhead light is essential.
3 • Storage units: Make sure light is directed inside hard-to-see places, so you can reach into drawers and cupboards and easily find what you're looking for.

86

feature lighting

As its name suggests, feature lighting in the bathroom is intended to illuminate specific aspects of the design. You might want strategically placed lights to draw attention to special features, from a monolithic bath in the centre of the room to a small ornament on a display shelf.

the bath

Consider panelling the bath with Perspex or a similar translucent acrylic, and backlighting this with fully protected strip lighting. The effect can be particularly striking if coloured acrylic is used. Another option is a perimeter of light at the base of a freestanding bath, created using recessed strips or even a ropelight. This will give the visual illusion of the bath floating in space.

the basin

Light directed at, and bouncing off, a high-gloss white ceramic basin is not as effective as light actually directed through a basin. With a glass bowl (or even just a glass basin surround), use recessed and waterproofed under-lighting to create a wonderful ethereal glow around the glass.

glass screens

As with basins, glass screens are ideal candidates for feature lighting. A wall of glass blocks or a shower screen of green-tinged frosted glass can be up-lit or down-lit. The light streams along and through the glass, and hangs tantalisingly on the edges.

display shelves and alcoves

Passing light, from either above or below, through a series of glass shelves brings a stunning luminance to the display area. You might also want to highlight any alcoves or recesses in the bathroom wall.

87 the heat is on

As you step out of a hot bath or steamy shower, the last thing you want is to be greeted by a chill in the air. Radiators and underfloor heating will create a welcoming ambient temperature, but if you've never encountered underfloor heating before, it may feel like a bit of risk choosing to install it. How do you decide between the two types of heating?

now you see it . . .

5 ideas

Do you want a visible radiator or concealed underfloor heating? Radiators are either ugly eyesores or style statements – but neither is discreet. underfloor heating, on the other hand, is hidden beneath your floor finish and you can't tell it's there until you walk barefoot over it.

saving space?

If you need to free up wall space, underfloor heating seems like the better option. But you'll still need a rail to hang your towels. Sometimes a small radiator hung high on the wall over the bath, for example, is equally space-saving.

economic situation

Underfloor heating gives out radiant heat, transmitting heat directly to cooler surfaces, such as your body. Radiators heat by convection; warm air rises, becomes cold and falls, creating air currents and hot and cold patches. As radiant heat is more effective, it can be used at lower temperatures and can be cheaper to run than a radiator.

fresh air

Underfloor heating doesn't create air movement, so it's a healthier option than radiators for asthmatics or anyone who is susceptible to allergies. This is because there's no continuous circulation of dust in the air.

maintenance

Yes, a radiator will be easier to access than underfloor heating. However, with electric underfloor heating most manufacturers offer a 10-year guarantee and can pinpoint faults so only a few tiles need to be lifted. A leak in a water-based system is much more of a problem.

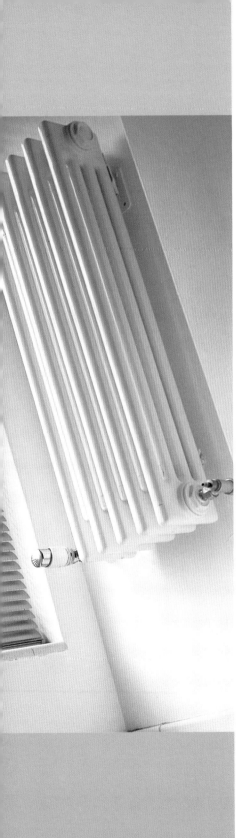

underfloor heating

There are two main types of underfloor heating: hydronic and electric.

hydronic

A hydronic system consists of a network of hot water pipes laid in a concrete screed floor. If you're simply renovating a bathroom, a hydronic system probably isn't suitable:

• it would elevate the floor by about 15cm (creating a big step at the threshold);
• the concrete would be too heavy for your joists;
• it's very expensive to install.

However, if you're building a new house and want underfloor heating throughout, a hot water system is the best solution (it's cheap to run in the long-term).

electric

Electrical underfloor heating comes in three main forms:

• Foil mats: panels of extremely thin, tightly woven carbon or metal mesh.
• Cable mats: electrical cables are set at regular intervals within a fibre-glass mesh. They require a regular-shaped room as the cabling can't be cut.
• Cabling: electrical cabling gives more flexibility to reach areas that the cable mats can't.

Foil mats are low voltage and have low heat-output, which means they can be used with wood, laminate and vinyl floors, as well as stone and ceramic. They don't produce enough heat to be the sole source in the room, whereas cable mats and cabling can be either the primary or secondary heat source in the room, depending on the heat output. The higher outputs are best suited to stone and ceramic flooring.

Electrical systems are just a few millimetres high and can be taped onto the subfloor and then covered with the floor adhesive, before the tiles are laid. The systems are insulated and waterproofed for safety.

radiators

For the style-conscious homeowner, the flat-panelled, enamel-painted, standard radiator is no longer to be tolerated. Radiators are now recognised as aesthetic focal points in the room, rather than unattractive necessities.

modern

Contemporary designs include ladder rails and loops, curves and squares, as well as abstract geometry. Many styles double up as towel warmers, although their primary function is to heat the room. The latest trends are:

• Metallic finishes such as matt or polished chrome to coordinate with taps and other accessories

• Tall, thin, vertical designs – wall-mounted to make floors easier to clean and free up space for the bath and other fixtures

• Integrated accessories such as mirrors, robe hooks and even shelving

traditional

Aficionados of vintage chic have revived interest in the classic, cast-iron column radiator. It offers a robust elegance, though does take up a lot of room. An alternative style is the ball-jointed ladder in brass, nickel or mixage finishes (see 55), with cross-head or ceramic valves to add an authentic look. Like its contemporary cousins, it can be wall-mounted and is more space saving than a column style of radiator.

hot enough?

Estimating the optimum radiator size and heat output needed for a room is a job best left to a professional. Precise calculations can take into account not only the room size, but also the size of windows, double-glazing, and the number and area of outside walls.

fuel for thought

Most radiators can be plumbed into your gas central-heating system, but some are electric only, and others offer the flexibility of dual-fuel. Electric models can be operated independently, so that even in the summer, you can keep the bathroom warmer than the rest of the house.

towel warmers

In bathroom design, the terms radiator and towel warmer are often seen as interchangeable, but strictly speaking, a towel warmer does not emit enough heat to warm a room. As the name suggests, its purpose is to dry and warm towels. For this reason, ladder designs are the most common, as towels can be conveniently hung over the rungs to dry.

Towel warmers are usually operated electrically, and are independent of the central-heating system so you can still have comfortably warm towels during the summer months when the heating is switched off.

doubling up

towel warmers and radiators

A heated towel rail may seem redundant if there's a radiator in the bathroom, but often the radiator is not suitable for drying or warming towels: either because of its shape or perhaps it's too far from the bath. In which case, it makes sense to supplement the radiator with a ladder-style towel warmer, mounted above the bath, for example. But you can find radiators and heated towel rails integrated into one unit, usually in a traditional style: a column radiator in the middle with a ball-jointed towel rail framing it.

towel warmers and underfloor heating

If you have underfloor heating, you'll have nowhere to dry your towels in the bathroom. In which case, a towel warmer is an excellent solution – but not so hot that it will overheat the bathroom.

size matters

When choosing a towel warmer, take into account the size of your towels. If you have large bath sheets, choose a wider model, so the towels won't have to be folded up too much to fit on it.

finishing touches

The smallest details really do make a difference. If you've spent time, energy and money creating your perfect bathroom, it's a shame if the design falls at the last hurdle. So when you're renovating your bathroom, remember the small, but practical, accessories that will make life easier – and your bathroom truly perfect.

toothbrush holder

A rack or cup, either wall-mounted or freestanding, offers room to store several toothbrushes – and the toothpaste too. But be sure to check whether the holes will take your usual brand of toothbrush: sometimes, chunky handles don't fit through.

toilet brush

An essential companion to the WC, the loo brush comes in all styles, from sleek polished chrome to funky colourful plastic. Look for models that hide the brush from sight and have an easy-to-clean interior and exterior.

soap dish or dispenser

If you use a bar of soap, keep it to hand in a rack-style or ridged dish that will allow the underside of the soap to dry. For liquid soap, consider a wall-mounted pump dispenser, which clears the counter of yet another bottle.

robe hooks

Your dressing gown needs a home, and a robe hook on the back of the bathroom door is the perfect place.

towel hoops or rails

If your basin doesn't offer an integrated rack, make sure you provide a convenient hoop or rail to hold the hand-towel. In addition, if you don't have a suitable radiator or towel warmer, you'll need longer rails to drape bath sheets over.

5 details

92 mirrors

In a bathroom, mirrors perform several functions: one is, obviously, as a looking glass. But as well as this, a mirror is a useful means of enhancing light in a dark bathroom, and it also serves to visually increase the dimensions of a small space.

up close and personal

Fixed flush to the wall or on the front of a cabinet, your looking-glass needs to offer good balanced lighting so your face isn't in shadow, which means you'll need light at least from either side, if not all directions.

For 'close-up work', such as putting on eye make-up, plucking hairs or putting in contact lenses, a supplementary magnifying mirror with integrated illumination is an extremely useful addition. Fitted to a flexible stem, it can be angled to best advantage.

optical illusions

An expanse of mirror can be positioned to reflect natural light, or even artificial light sources, into dark corners. Not only will a wall-to-wall mirror above the bath achieve this, but it will also seem to double the size of your room. Be sure though that you'll feel comfortable with a large mirror in the bathroom: not everyone likes to see themselves so exposed.

steamy mirrors

One problem with mirrors in a bathroom is that they tend to become fogged up when you have a steamy shower, or even a hot bath. An anti-condensation coating helps reduce the problem, but the best solution is to raise the temperature of the mirrored surface so steam can't condense there. Some mirrors come with an integrated heating element, and you can also buy thin heating pads to fix behind wall mirrors, which take the chill off the surface.

93

towels wrap yourself in comfort

Who used to think twice about towels? They were there to dry yourself with after you washed your face or stepped out of the bath or shower. Now, however, they play an aesthetic role, enhancing the design of the bathroom – and in this age of pampering, have psychological value, making us feel cocooned in luxury and softness.

Most towels are made from soft and absorbent cotton, with some of the most luxurious being woven from 100% Egyptian cotton, which is renowned for its ultra-long, fine fibres. You might also find cotton mixed with linen (for durability and elegance), modal (for greater softness and absorbency) and silk (for sheer indulgence).

Texture is very important with towels. A flat towel has less surface area and therefore isn't as effective at drying. Terry towelling is so popular because it has thousands of fibres that each absorb water. The disadvantage of these projecting fibres is that they tend to catch on things and pull. For a softer feel than towelling, you can find cotton velour or combed cotton, and for a very contemporary look, choose ribbed

designs and waffle-weaves, which are more durable – though less soft on the skin.

Colour-wise, you may want to match your towels to your decor or make them an accent colour against white sanitaryware. White offers a beautiful crisp look when it's freshly laundered, but white hand towels never stay pristine for long. Aqueous shades of blue and green, or neutrals like taupe, grey and mushroom are currently popular. It's worth noting that plain colours will stand the test of time longer than patterns.

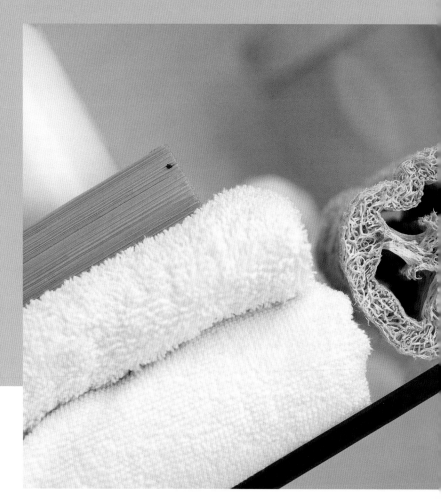

94 lotions and potions

Where once we used to hide away our bottles and tubs and tubes and pots, or leave them scattered higgledy-piggledy around the bath and basin, now it's not unusual to see them used as aesthetic accessories, adding the finishing touch to a bathroom design. Display your toiletries on shelves, in recesses, in a neat row alongside the bath, and consider them accents to your overall design.

judging by appearances

You may buy your shampoo because it makes your hair feel really clean or you like how it smells – but the truly design-conscious homeowner selects a bottle of shampoo for its good looks. Shampoos, conditioners, shower gels, bath oils and soaps come in packaging to suit all tastes – and all types of bathrooms. You can also get the same effect by decanting your favourite products into matching containers.

- Minimal: plain white bottles and tubes, with as little writing on as possible
- Organic: greens and brown; raw corrugated cardboard-wrapped bottles
- Industrial: grey and black or even aluminium packaging; chunky shapes
- Colourful: zesty plastics and brightly hued glass
- Traditional: old-fashioned, pharmacy-style glass bottles

practically speaking

Think about the practicalities as well as the aesthetics when buying your toiletries. First of all, a large glass bottle may look lovely, but it'll be very slippery in wet hands, and certainly isn't safe around children. It's liable to shatter if dropped, leaving you treading barefoot around slivers of glass. And if it's heavy enough, it's likely to crack or chip your ceramic tiles or basin. Beware too of some metal bottles – surprisingly, they are not all rust-proof and you could be left with rusty stains that are difficult to remove.

95
window treatments

Although you may sometimes want a darkened bathroom for a relaxing bath, usually you want it to be a light and fresh space where you can make good use of the mirror. Weigh your need for natural light against your desire for privacy.

glazing over

It's possible to have your windowpanes professionally sandblasted or acid-etched, or covered with a frosted film, or even replaced with patterned glass. This gives a degree of opacity, but still allows plenty of light to enter.

a different perspective

Angle Venetian blinds to allow light in but keep prying eyes out. For example, if your bathroom is on the second floor of a house, tilt the slats upwards so to the passer-by below they present a closed face, but the sun can shine down into the room.

sheer beauty

If the bathroom does not get too humid, consider fabric window dressings. A new generation of sheers has replaced old-fashioned and fussy net curtains. Airy and light, they add a soft and romantic touch to a bathroom.

panel judgment

Running on top and bottom tracks, panels slide across the window to control light or the view. A popular look is the Japanese-style wooden grid with waxed shoji paper or translucent acrylic insets.

half measures

Consider covering only the bottom half of your window. This can be done not only with curtains or sheers, but also with roller blinds that run upwards, or with half-shutters that can be left closed for privacy, while light streams in above.

5 ideas

the door 96

As the entryway to your bathroom, the door is an important part of the design, and you might want to renovate or replace the door when you fit your new bathroom.

panelled doors

If you have a traditional panelled door, but a modern bathroom design, consider creating a contemporary look by covering the panelled fascia with a flat veneer. It's cheaper than replacing a whole door.

tropical wood doors

Unpainted wooden doors are perfect for organic-looking bathrooms, and dark tropical wood gives an exotic look. As solid hardwoods are expensive (and not always eco-friendly), simply dark-stain a blond, softwood door. Several applications will hide knotholes and grain, to create a chic, tropical-hardwood look.

frameless glass doors

You'll need an expert glazier to make a toughened glass door that meets all safety requirements. As toughened glass can't be cut without shattering, ensure the measurements are precise to the millimetre (have you taken account of your new flooring, for example?) and that holes are pre-cut for the handles. And make sure the door is frosted, if you want privacy!

dress it up

Update an old door with new handles. If you have slick matt-chrome taps, choose pared-down, matt-chrome door handles. Likewise, if your bathroom is traditional, a decorative brass handle and door plate will be more fitting.

lockdown

In a family home, a lock on the bathroom door may seem unnecessary. But think about your poor guests who might not welcome accidental interruptions! If you're wary about adding a lock for fear that your children might get trapped inside, you could use a simple bolt placed high on the door where little ones can't reach it.

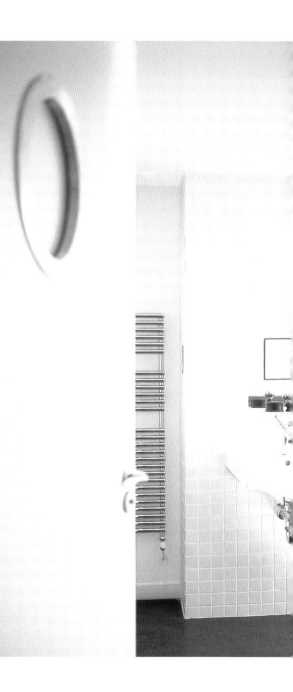

3

part three

keeping it fresh

97

easy-care bathrooms

Considering the amount of water in a bathroom (not to mention soap), it's amazing how dirty the surfaces get! Although effective at cleaning our bodies, water is actually the prime culprit when it comes to soiling the bathroom. Water droplets adhere to all the surfaces they touch and run over, leaving behind traces of limescale, dirt, germs and soapy residue.

You can protect your bathroom – and cut down on the time you spend cleaning – by installing products that are specially designed to be low-maintenance, as well as by employing design concepts that make the room generally easy to look after.

clean lines

Using sanitaryware with simple lines, rounded edges and smooth surfaces reduces awkward angles where dirt can hide. Avoid decorative details where dust will settle and bacteria can get trapped.

10 ideas

matt surfaces

Limescale dulls the gleam of polished surfaces and watermarks show up more on gloss finishes. Choose matt or satin finishes on your taps, shower fittings, ceramic tiles and lacquered furniture to disguise marks.

special glazes

Many manufacturers offer proprietary anti-adhesive glazes on their ceramic WCs and basins. These coatings repel water so it slides away, taking all deposits with it. You can also find water-repellent coatings to reduce unsightly marks on shower doors and bath screens.

integrated antibacterial properties

Some materials, such as linoleum and wood, have a natural resistance to bacteria. The linseed oil in linoleum emits a gas that kills microbes, while tests on many species of wood, such as teak, oak, maple and sycamore, have demonstrated the efficiency of wood's inherent defence system against bacteria and fungus.

covered storage

Display shelves and open surfaces look attractive, but they are a natural place for dirt

and dust to gather. And cleaning is no fun when you have to pick up bottles, tubs and a multitude of objects first. Cabinets with doors are more practical and allow you to hide away clutter (see 67).

wall-mounting

Fixing the WC, basin and even furniture units to the wall (see 13) keeps the floor space clear so it's easier to mop it. In addition, there are no pedestals or legs where dirt can linger unseen. Also consider wall-mounting your taps, as this prevents water pooling around the base of the tap and creating a ring of limescale.

seamless surfaces

Where two different surfaces meet, the join can harbour bacteria and dirt, for example, where a ceramic basin is inset in a stone vanity counter. You can eliminate this difficult-to-clean area by using seamless surfaces, such as a glass, stone or composite counter with an integrated basin (see 47 and 48).

in-built countermeasures

Choose showerheads with limescale defences, such as pins that push through the holes to prevent them blocking up (see 42). And make sure your whirlpool bath has a self-clean system that, for example, flushes the pipes with disinfectant (see 34).

low-maintenance flooring

Stone and wood may be beautiful, but they do require occasional maintenance to re-seal them. Choose materials that are hardwearing and don't require much care, such as vinyl or linoleum on a roll (see 77 to 82).

water softener

To eliminate the problem of limescale if you live in a hard-water area, consider getting a water softener fitted to your system. This counteracts the limescale so you can be sure your bathroom remains as good as new.

98
on-going maintenance

You'll want to keep your bathroom spotless and hygienic, but don't be tempted to get out the scouring brush. Check manufacturers' or suppliers' guidelines on cleaning and treat all surfaces with care. You can damage them with too much attention, as well as too little.

• Acrylic: don't use harsh, acidic or abrasive detergents – a soft sponge and mild detergent will suffice.
• Ceramic: use a non-abrasive cream or spray detergent on sanitaryware and wall tiles, and mop floors with mild disinfectant. Rinse floors so they're neither sticky nor slippery.
• Composites: wipe clean using a damp cloth and mild detergent. You can polish out scratches with micro-textured sandpaper.
• Enamel: use a gentle spray or cream cleaner and wet sponge or cloth to remove grime from inside your roll-top bath.
• Glass: proprietary glass and mirror cleaners strip the surface of unsightly smears and finger marks. Use a lint-free cloth to avoid leaving tiny fibres on the surface.
• Laminate: although the edges of laminated furniture should be well sealed, avoid using a very wet cloth in case water seeps in. Use furniture polish and a dry cloth instead.
• Metal: avoid acid-based cleaners that cause tarnish. Most mild cleansers will be suitable or choose specialist cleansers for brass, chrome, steel etc, and soft micro-fibre cloths to restore brightness.
• Paintwork: use furniture polish or a wet cloth on gloss paint, but avoid dampening other paints, even satin-finish paint, unless necessary to remove a mark.
• Stone: follow suppliers' instructions regarding re-sealing. Use a damp cloth or mop on polished surfaces, and scrub textured ones with a soft brush and mild detergent. Brush stone floors regularly to remove abrasive dirt.
• Wood: you can wax or polish wood as appropriate. Wooden baths and basins will need to be re-sealed occasionally with a soap solution or oil.

changing the look

Your project has finished, a year has passed, and you realise you're bored with your bathroom. It's time to update it without causing major damage – you're certainly not prepared for the financial or emotional strain of a complete revamp yet. So what else can you do?

wall finishes

One advantage of painting your walls is that it's extremely simple to re-paint, so why not just choose a different colour and pick up the paintbrush? Changing the tiles will be more expensive and messier (and make sure they don't damage anything as they fall), but for a radical new look, it could be worth it.

flooring

Lay lino or vinyl on your wooden floor, take up the high-maintenance stone and replace with rubber, remove the tiles with the dirty grout and replace with bamboo. In some cases, it may be tricky to put down a new floor covering as it will involve cutting intricate shapes, but if your fixtures are wall-hung, life will be much simpler.

centrepiece

Maybe your room lacks a focal point – or you're tired of the one that's there. Replace your basin or bath with something a little unusual – swap ceramic for glass, or acrylic for wood. If you select something of the same shape and size, re-decoration will be minimised.

details

Small details such as the taps and shower fittings can make a big difference. Exchange brass for chrome or contemporary for traditional, but make sure that you choose similar types (three-hole mixers, for example) unless you want to have to re-plumb.

accessories

Strip away your current accessories like towels, bath mats and any ornaments and replace with a new set, coordinated for a whole new look: whether it's a bright colour or a muted shade, it will revitalise the bathroom.

plants and flowers how green
is your bathroom?

The bathroom, particularly if it's dressed with modern materials, can sometimes seem cold, hard-edged and unwelcoming. There's no better way to enliven it than by adding something organic. Whether you turn your bathroom into a faux-jungle or simply display a single stem, the addition of plants and flowers will add a softer note – a breath of life.

When looking for plants for a bathroom, bear in mind humidity and light levels. Most bathrooms will be warm and humid places, where exotic species like bamboo and banana plants will thrive. In limited natural light, choose varieties of fern and ivy, ficus and philodendron, and rotate plants towards the light so they don't grow in one direction. Use small plants like cacti (which won't need watering at all in the damp atmosphere) or even bonsai trees along the windowsill or on shelves for stylish displays. Larger, broad-leafed species can be used as a window treatment to prevent prying eyes peering in.

Add colour to the bathroom with potted flowering plants such as begonias, letting them trail in a hanging basket over the bath. Other potted flowers such as orchids are perfect for a minimalist look and add an elegance and pure form in keeping with the design.

Finally, for a burst of colour or to freshen the air, display cut flowers in a series of small vases (though note that they may wilt a little if the bathroom is too warm). As petals drop off, why not scatter them in your bathwater in a romantic gesture?

fresh air

Commonly used plants in bathrooms, such as spider plants, bamboo, philodendrons and ivy, are not just decorative but also remove pollutants from the air and replace them with oxygen. The peace lily, the humble chrysanthemum, the gerbera daisy and the areca palm also have air-filtering properties, and will help rid the bathroom of toxins from formaldehyde (in MDF, for example), benzene (plastics and rubber) and trichloroethylene (paints).

101

relax or revive
with the power
of scent

index

acknowledgements

Author's acknowledgements

My thanks go to Jane O'Shea, Hilary Mandleberg, Helen Lewis, Paul Welti and Samantha Rolfe at Quadrille for all their help and hard work in seeing this book come to completion. And, of course, to my husband, Michael, for his support in my freelance career.

Picture credits

1 Ray Main/Mainstream; 7 Ray Main/Mainstream/Arch Julie Richards@msn.com; 8-9 Ray Main/Mainstream; 10-11 Ray Main/Mainstream/ Dev Martin Lee Associates; 12-13 Ray Main/Mainstream/Hemmingway designs; 14-15 Ray Main/Mainstream/Arch Julie Richards@msn.com; 16 Ray Main/Mainstream; 18-19 Ray Main/Mainstream/Developer Leeds Loft Co.; 20 Main/Mainstream/Guinevere; 21 Ray Main/Mainstream/MMR Architects; 22 Ray Main/Mainstream/Architect Spencer Fung; 23 Ray Main/Mainstream; 24 Ray Main/Mainstream; 24-25 Ray Main/Mainstream; 26 Ray Main/Mainstream; 27 Ray Main/Mainstream; 29 Ray Main/Mainstream/Designer Roger Oates; 30-31 Ray Main/Mainstream; 31 Ray Main/Mainstream/Hazlitts; 32-33 Ray Main/Mainstream; 35 Ray Main/Mainstream; 26-37 Ray Main/Mainstream/C2 Architects; 37 Ray Main/Mainstream; 38 above Ray Main/Mainstream; 38 below Ray Main/Mainstream/Developers Candy&Candy; 40 Ray Main/Mainstream/Architects Gregory Phillips; 41 Ideal-Standard Idealcast roll top bath www.ideal-standard.co.uk; 42 Ray Main/Mainstream; 42-43 inset Ray Main/Mainstream/Patel Taylor Architects; 43 Ray Main/Mainstream/Developer Candy&Candy; 44-45 Ray Main/Mainstream/Architect Neil Fletchers; 46-47 Ray Main/Mainstream; 48 Alchemy showerhead by Sottini (an Ideal-Standard company) www.sottini.co.uk; 49 Darren Chung/Mainstream; 50 Ray Main/Mainstream; 51 Ray Main/Mainstream/Developer Candy&Candy; 52 below Darren Chung/Mainstream; 52-3 above Ray Main/Mainstream/Architect Simon Conder; 53 below Ray Main/Mainstream/John Minshaw Designs; 54-55 Ray Main/Mainstream; 56 below Ray Main/Mainstream/Designer Andrew Martin; 56 above Ray Main/Mainstream; 57 centre Ray Main/Mainstream/ Candy&Candy; 57 right Ray Main/Mainstream; 57 left Darren Chung/Mainstream/C2 Design; 59 Ray Main/Mainstream/John Minshaw Designs; 60-61 Ray Main/Mainstream/London & Country Homes; 62 top Ray Main/Mainstream/Designer Paul Daly; 62 below Ray Main/Mainstream; 63 above Ray Main/Mainstream; 63 below Ray Main/Mainstream/ The Rookery; 64 Ray Main/Mainstream/Developers Candy&Candy; 65 Dreamworks three-hole basin mixer by Michael Graves for Dornbracht www.dornbracht.com; 66 Ray Main/Mainstream; 67 Sottini Cresta suite www.sottini.co.uk; 68-69 Ray Main/Mainstream/ Mary Thum Architects; 68-69 inset Ray Main/Mainstream/ Arch Wells Mackereth; 70-71 Ray Main/Mainstream; 72 Ray Main/Mainstream; 73 Ray Main/Mainstream/Architect Sabrina Foster; 74 Ray Main/Mainstream; 75 Ray Main/Mainstream; 76-7 main & inset Ray Main/Mainstream/ Abraham & Thakore; 78-79 Ray Main/Mainstream; 79 Ray Main/Mainstream; 80 Ray Main/Mainstream/Architect Charles Rutherford; 80-81 Ray Main/Mainstream; 81 Ray Main/Mainstream; 82-83 main Ray Main/Mainstream; 82-3 inset Ray Main/Mainstream; 84-85 Ray Main/Mainstream; 87 Darren Chung/Mainstream/ Bathaus; 88-89 Ray Main/Mainstream; 89 Ray Main/Mainstream; 90-91 Ray Main/Mainstream/John Minshaw Designs; 91 Ray Main/Mainstream/Designer Gianni Cinnali; 92 Darren Chung/Mainstream/Bathaus; 93 Ray Main/Mainstream; 94-95 Ray Main/Mainstream; 96-97 Ray Main/Mainstream; 98 Ray Main/Mainstream; 99 Ray Main/Mainstream/Designer Nick Allen; 100-101 Ray Main/Mainstream; 102-103 Darren Chung/Mainstream; 103 Ray Main/Mainstream; 104 Ray Main/Mainstream; 105 Ray Main/Mainstream; 106 Ray Main/Mainstream; 107 Ray Main/Mainstream/Designer Catherine Memmi; 108 Ray Main/Mainstream/MMR Architects; 109 Ray Main/Mainstream; 111 Ray Main/Mainstream; 112-113 Ray Main/Mainstream/Gregory Phillips; 114-115 Darren Chung/Mainstream/C2 Design; 116 Ray Main/Mainstream; 117 Ray Main/Mainstream